the scrapbook *Embellishment* handbook

by
Sherry Steveson

MEMORY MAKERS BOOKS

CINCINNATI, OHIO

www.memorymakersmagazine.com
www.mycraftivity.com

The Scrapbook Embellishment Handbook. Copyright© 2009 by Sherry Steveson. Manufactured in China. All rights reserved. It is permissible for the purchaser to make the projects contained herein and sell them at fairs, bazaars and craft shows. No other part of this book may be reproduced in any form or by any electronic or mechanical means including information storage and retrieval systems without permission in writing from the publisher, except by a reviewer, who may quote a brief passage in review. Published by Memory Makers Books, an imprint of F+W Media, Inc., 4700 East Galbraith Road, Cincinnati, Ohio 45236. (800) 289-0963. First edition.

13 12 11 10 09   5 4 3 2 1

Distributed in Canada by Fraser Direct
100 Armstrong Avenue
Georgetown, ON, Canada L7G 5S4
Tel: (905) 877-4411

Distributed in the U.K. and Europe by David & Charles
Brunel House, Newton Abbot, Devon, TQ12 4PU, England
Tel: (+44) 1626 323200, Fax: (+44) 1626 323319
E-mail: postmaster@davidandcharles.co.uk

Distributed in Australia by Capricorn Link
P.O. Box 704, S. Windsor, NSW 2756 Australia
Tel: (02) 4577-3555

Library of Congress Cataloging-in-Publication Data

Steveson, Sherry.
   The scrapbook embellishmer.t handbook / Sherry Steveson. -- 1st ed.
      p. cm.
   Includes index.
   ISBN 978-1-59963-035-9 (pbk. : alk. paper)
   1. Photograph albums--Handbooks, manuals, etc. 2. Scrapbooking--Handbooks, manuals, etc. 3. Handicraft--Handbooks, manuals, etc. 4. Decoration and ornament--Handbooks, manuals, etc. I. Title.
   TR501.S738 2009
   745.593--dc22
                              2008055199

www.fwmedia.com

EDITOR: **KRISTIN BOYS**

DESIGNER: **KELLY O'DELL**

PRODUCTION COORDINATOR:
MATT WAGNER

PHOTOGRAPHERS:
**RIC DELIANTONI, AL PARRISH,
CHRISTINE POLOMSKY,
ADAM HAND**

STYLIST: **JAN NICKUM**

Metric Conversion Chart

to convert	to	multiply by
Inches	Centimeters	2.54
Centimeters	Inches	0.4
Feet	Centimeters	30.5
Centimeters	Feet	0.03
Yards	Meters	0.9
Meters	Yards	1.1
Sq. Inches	Sq. Centimeters	6.45
Sq. Centimeters	Sq. Inches	0.16
Sq. Feet	Sq. Meters	0.09
Sq. Meters	Sq. Feet	10.8
Sq. Yards	Sq. Meters	0.8
Sq. Meters	Sq. Yards	1.2
Pounds	Kilograms	0.45
Kilograms	Pounds	2.2
Ounces	Grams	28.3
Grams	Ounces	0.035

ABOUT THE AUTHOR

Sherry Steveson has been passionate about scrapbooking for over 10 years. Finding a hobby that merged her love for photography with her gift of writing, all wrapped up in a creative outlet was the catalyst for a lifelong devotion. Her work has been published in many of the major scrapbook magazines and idea books, and she is the author of *When Life Gives You Lemons* (Memory Makers Books, 2008). It always brings a thrill to her family when they see their faces on the pages of those publications. She has also found her calling teaching scrapbooking to others. Sherry currently maintains a blog at www.sherrysteveson.typepad. com. When she isn't writing, scrapbooking or teaching, she keeps a busy schedule with her three children, her husband's landscape business and training to run a marathon.

dedication

I would like to dedicate this book to my husband, Jason, who has supported another journey down this road of writing and creating. His endless supply of foot rubs and enduring my late nights is exactly what I needed from my best friend.

To Jacob, Madison and Fletcher, who continue to be an extension of my own heart, for making my journey of life worthwhile and fun.

To my parents and sister, for all your belief and support.

To all the scrapbookers I have come to know over the years that have mentioned their desire for a book like this, I hope I have fulfilled your wishes.

acknowledgments

I couldn't have done this without the confidence that Christine Doyle and Kristin Boys placed in me. It has been a complete pleasure to work with you again on this endeavor.

I appreciate the hard work and talent of my contributors: Kimber McGray, Nic Howard, Suzy Plantamura, Jamie Harper, Rita Weiss, Cindy Tobey, Melissa Phillips, Judi VanValkinburg, Stephanie Vetne, Janet Ohlson and Katrina Simeck.

TABLE OF CONTENTS

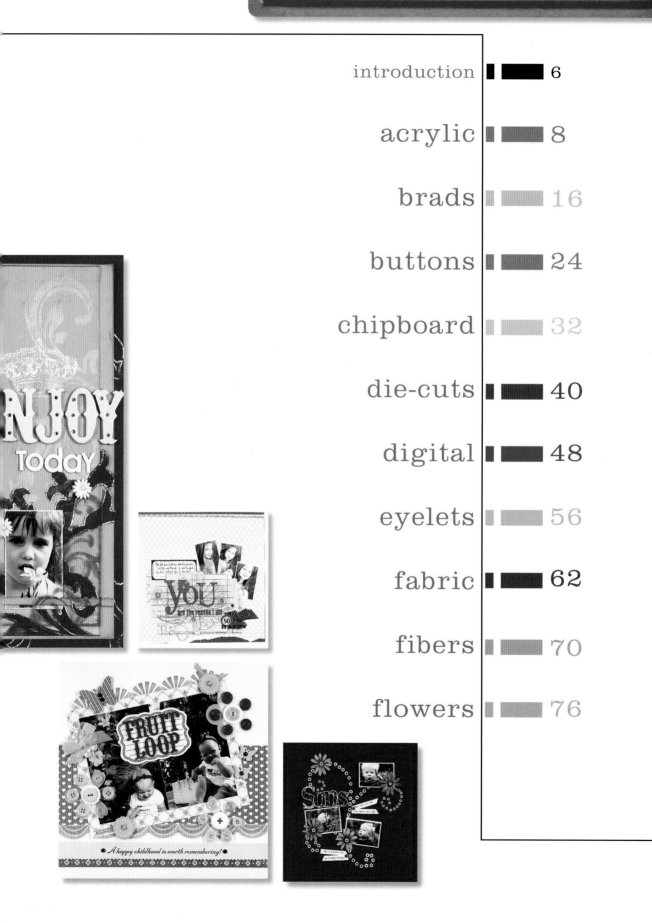

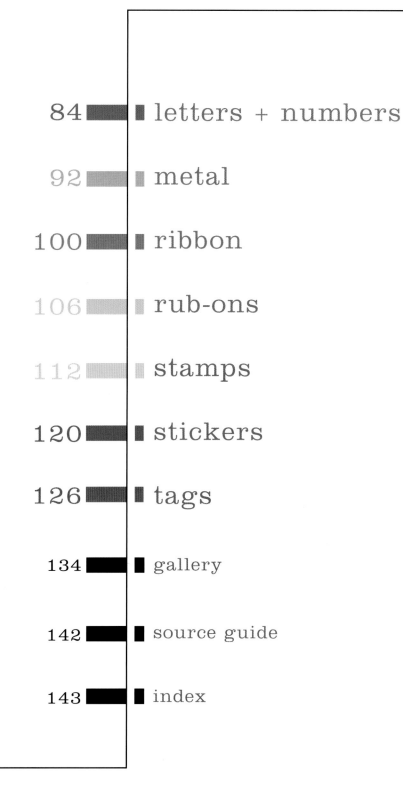

Ask any scrapbooker one thing they love about the hobby and many will say shopping for it. Shopping for supplies is as much fun as using the supplies themselves. Ironically, what plagues many of us is an overabundance of gorgeous trinkets and embellishments. Oodles of supplies can leave us overwhelmed and frustrated over what to do with it all. What we need is a resource full of fresh ideas and solutions for using embellishments. This book is designed to be just that—a guide to using common embellishments, providing inspiration for breathing new life into these supplies.

introduction

This handbook is divided into 17 sections, each covering a different type of embellishment. I want you to use this book as a reference you go back to again and again. Each section illustrates several ways to use your embellishments in creative ways. Start by trying out the ideas yourself, and then use them as starting points for ideas of your own. In addition to the layouts, I'll show you how to complete three of the techniques in each section. These step-by-step techniques are divided into three levels designed to follow you as you grow in your creativity: Simply Create (1), Kick It Up (2) and Think Outside the Box (3). Simply Create techniques are meant for embellishment beginners and illustrate a simple technique for using embellishments. No matter what your skill level, Kick It Up techniques will show you how to take your embellishments to the next level. And Think Outside the Box techniques will get you thinking beyond the obvious way to use embellishments and take your creativity to a new dimension. Most of the illustrated techniques in the book are simple, requiring fewer than four steps, so however creative you're getting, you can still scrap in a flash.

My intention is for this book to grow with you as you acquire scrapbooking skills, and for you to find it will provide tried and true ideas that will stand the test of time. Whenever you get stuck for an idea, pull out the book. When you want to try something new, flip it open. When you want to use up your stash, pour over this book page by page. Keep it on your desk for quick reference. Wear out the binding! It will be your best tool for embellishing your pages.

acrylic

It's clear: Acrylic is one of the hottest scrapbook materials to emerge in recent years. Acrylic embellishments come in nearly every shape and size imaginable. Its unique quality is what makes it so popular. Paper and chipboard can't compete with clear plastic for sheer intrigue. And acrylic's transparent nature makes it possible to layer elements in ways you can't achieve with traditional materials. Acrylic works well paired with solvent inks, paint, rub-ons and more. The ideas in this section are just the tip of the acrylic iceberg but will provide a foundation on which to build.

DRESS WITH DECORATIVE TAPE

Decorative tape easily dresses up clear acrylic shapes. Simply place the ribbon in the desired pattern over the top of the shape. Leaving areas of the acrylic uncovered allows the photos to show through. You can also add rub-ons to the acrylic. This acrylic star makes a great backdrop for the title of this page about my skateboarding daredevil son, Fletcher.

Supplies: Cardstock (Prism); decorative tape, rub-ons (Heidi Swapp); acrylic (Pageframes); bookplate (Junkitz); adhesive (3M, Glue Dots)

LAYER TRANSPARENCIES IN A FRAME

Layering several preprinted transparencies under a piece of clear acrylic transforms a basic shape into custom art. Use a piece like this as a dimensional background for a layout or as a page in a mini album. Here, Judi designed a one-of-a-kind photo frame to show off a collage of her favorite family photos as a work of art.

Supplies: Acrylic frame, title accent (Pageframes); transparency (Hambly, Luxe); stamps (7gypsies); flowers (Prima); glitter (Art Institute, Ranger); ribbon (Cloud 9) brad (Creative Imaginations); adhesives (3M, Glue Dots, Tombow, Tsukineko)

Artwork by Judi VanValkinburg

Make acrylic flowers pop

Nic is an expert at creating layers on a page. To give this layout dimension, Nic bent her acrylic flowers so they pop off the page. You can use this layering technique with multiple layers of any shape of acrylic. The result is a fantastic 3-D quality that makes you want to reach out and touch the page.

Supplies: Cardstock (Bazzill); patterned paper (Autumn Leaves, Making Memories, Teresa Collins); die-cut paper (Making Memories); transparency (My Mind's Eye, Rhonna Designs); brads (Queen & Co.); flowers (Heidi Swapp, Queen & Co.); hearts (Heidi Swapp)

materials
large acrylic flower

small acrylic flower

brad

hole punch (optional)

February 2008.

I followed you over to Jessie's to grab a few photos of you two together.

I managed to take a good amount of photos; these are just some of my favourite ones of you.

Artwork by Nic Howard

one

Using your forefinger and thumb, gently press each petal of the larger flower so it folds in half. Repeat with the smaller flower.

two

Stack the flowers and place a brad in the center to attach them. Punch a hole in the center of the flowers if needed.

STAMP WITH SOLVENT INK

Solvent ink is a waterproof ink that works best when used on nonporous surfaces. This makes solvent ink perfect for altering acrylic shapes! Jamie stamped these plain acrylic letters using black solvent ink to enhance this page about a friendship. The black pattern distinguishes the letters from the background. Experiment with different stamps and colors of ink to achieve a personalized look for your page.

Supplies: Cardstock (Bazzill); patterned paper (Scenic Route); acrylic letters (Heidi Swapp); transparency (Avery); stamp (Technique Tuesday); spray paint (Krylon); die-cut shapes, letter and accent stickers (Scenic Route)

Artwork by Jamie Harper

Artwork by Cindy Tobey

MAKE LETTERS "SNOW" CREATIVE

Another reason to love clear acrylic is the chance to make it into any color you want with a few brushes of paint. Painting the back of these letters with purple acrylic allowed Cindy to coordinate her title with the photos of her daughter in the snow. She took it up a notch and added white flakes texture gel to the top of her title to mimic the look of snow. This gel medium is sold at many craft stores and makes a great addition to any winter-themed page.

Supplies: Patterned paper (Making Memories); acrylic letters (Heidi Swapp); chipboard circles (Fancy Pants); transparency (3M); texture gel (Liquitex); Misc: acrylic paint, cotton, floss, pipe cleaners, staples

Emboss acrylic

There is something magical about the transformation that takes place when a shape is embossed—kind of like that special moment when a butterfly sits on your hand. Kimber embossed these acrylic butterflies to lend dimension and texture to the simple shapes. The subtle design of the butterflies keeps the focus on the the photos while reinforcing theme of the page.

Supplies: Patterned paper (Making Memories, Pink Paislee); chipboard letters (Imagination Project); letter stickers (Making Memories); acrylic accents (Pageframes); photo corners (Heidi Swapp); glitter (Doodlebug)

Artwork by Kimber McGray

materials

acrylic shape

embossing machine (such as Cuttlebug)

embossing template

one

Sandwich the acrylic shape between the layers of the embossing template.

two

Run the template through the embossing machine.

three

Remove the embossed acrylic shape and add it to your page.

Ink and embellish acrylic

You've now seen ribbon, solvent ink and paint added to acrylic. What could be left? Alcohol inks, of course! Applying one color, or even combining several colors for your own special mix, will add a nice tint to a clear acrylic shape. Take it to another level by mixing glitter and stamping on texture for added dimension. Top it all off with rub-ons and you have an altered acrylic piece that is a showcase embellishment. Attaching these kicked-up acrylic flowers to my page provided the special touch I was looking for to express the special relationship my daughter has with her dance teacher.

Supplies: Patterned paper (7gypsies, Chatterbox, Creative Imaginations, Dream Street, Jenni Bowlin); letters (Autumn Leaves, BasicGrey); acrylic accent (Pageframes); rub-ons (Tinkering Ink); adhesive (3M, Glue Dots); alcohol ink (Ranger)

QUICK TIP
Adhesive will show through acrylic, so attach pieces with clear liquid glue or a clear adhesive dot. Take advantage of clever concealing when necessary!

materials

- clear acrylic shape
- spray adhesive
- glitter
- alcohol ink
- rubber stamp
- rub-on
- craft stick

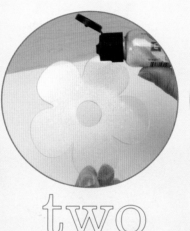

one

Coat the back of the acrylic shape with spray adhesive.

two

While the adhesive is still wet, sprinkle glitter over the wet adhesive. Tap any excess glitter off the shape.

three

Add drops of alcohol ink randomly in several spots on the front side of the acrylic shape.

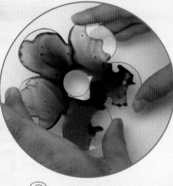

four

Tilt and bend the acrylic so that the ink spreads around the shape. Make sure the entire shape has color on it. Add additional ink as needed.

five

Using a clean stamp, "kiss" the stamp over the inked shape to remove some of the ink.

six

Allow the ink to dry. Then apply rub-ons to the front of the acrylic shape.

brads

Ahh ... the little brad. What started as an office supply staple has worked its way as a staple supply in many scrapbookers' stashes. While technically a fastener for attaching sheets of paper, the brad is actually so much more. Brads add instant depth, punch, texture and color to a page. They can stand in as simple bullet points on a page or dot a patterned paper flower. You can change a brad's hue using paint, embossing powders or flocking. Brads can be arranged in a variety of shapes and designs. You can layer brads with other embellishments. The brad's versatility makes is what makes it one of my favorite embellishments. Take a look at these ideas. I challenge you to make a "point" of using brads in all new ways.

MAKE A POINT

Kimber's idea to use brads to craft an exclamation point on her birthday card with brads conveys the enthusiasm of an entire birthday celebration. And dressing up one brad with a cupcake sticker really takes the cake! Using large brads to fashion a shape is simple and quick but really makes a statement. And the ideas are endless. Just sketch out the shape and insert away!

Artwork by Kimber McGray

Supplies: Cardstock (WorldWin); chipboard and sticker accents, patterned paper (KI Memories); brads (Heidi Swapp); ribbon (May Arts, Offray)

PLAY CONNECT THE DOTS

Cindy played with the idea of making shapes with her brads, then took it one step further. She wound red string around each little brad to play connect the dots. The swirling shape inspired ideas to swirl in my own head. For instance, make a flower with brads and connect the dots with yarn. Form a balloon and replace string with pen lines. Or fashion a star and connect the dots with glitter glue.

Supplies: Cardstock (Bazzill, WorldWin); letter stickers, journaling page, patterned paper, ribbon (Prima); brads (Queen & Co.); chipboard accents (American Crafts, BasicGrey); die-cut paper (KI Memories); adhesive (Glue Dots, Kokuyo, Stampin' Up); Misc: thread

Artwork by Cindy Tobey

Add letters to brads

Sometimes letter stickers need a little lift. Enter brads. For this layout, I trimmed individual letter stickers to fit on large brads. The brads act as a solid foundation for my title and enhance the statement. I altered the color of the brads before adding the letters (see page 23 for the how-to.), going with red, green and purple for a masculine birthday page that expresses my mixed feelings about my son getting older.

Supplies: Patterned paper (Sassafras Lass); acrylic shapes (Pageframes); letter stickers (American Crafts, EK Success); brads (American Crafts); Misc: ribbon

materials

letter stickers

scissors

brads

one

Cut letters to fit the size of your brads. Brads with a flat face work best.

two

Adhere letter stickers to the brads.

Artwork by Nic Howard

GET YOUR FILL OF BRADS

What I love about Nic's use of brads is that it's so simple but powerful and adds a charm to this page about her three children. Arranging tiny brads into a pattern that follows a preprinted design provides tons of texture. It also uses up a large stash of brads. On this page, Nic used brads to fill in a patterned paper shape, but die-cuts and stickers would also work. Mark where you want the brads to be before poking holes.

Supplies: Patterned paper (BasicGrey); rub-ons (Li'l Davis); stamps (Hero Arts); stickers (Making Memories); die-cut labels (Daisy D's); chipboard letters (CherryArte); paper punch (Fiskars); brads (Queen & Co.)

QUICK TIP
Use a thumbtack or needle to open a brad's tight, tiny prongs.

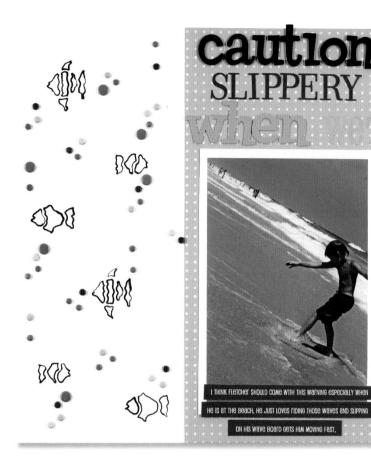

SUBSTITUTE BRADS FOR BUBBLES

My son reminds me of a fish when we are near the water. I decided that the fish stencil would be perfect for this page about his desire to ride the waves. I used brads to mimic bubbles floating around the fish and to provide a touch of color to the white background.

Supplies: Patterned paper (Scenic Route); letter stickers (American Crafts, Scenic Route); brads (American Crafts); brass stencil (Lasting Impressions)

EMBELLISH MESH WITH BRADS

On this layout, Suzy illustrates a fun way to embellish paper mesh with brads. The mesh acts as the template for randomly placing a variety of brads in the shape of little flowers. The look is as endearing as the precious girls featured on this page. It's whimsical and sweet—and easy to complete!

Supplies: Cardstock (Bazzill); patterned paper (We R Memory Keepers); brads (Junkitz, Making Memories, Queen & Co., unknown); mesh (Magic Mesh); chipboard letters (Prima); letter stickers (Making Memories); stickers (Adornit)

Artwork by Suzy Plantamura

Layer brads

brads

5 REASONS girls are fun

Love to shop

Will pose for pictures

Loves a good chick flick

Doesn't make as many messes

Can play as hard as the boys and still look pretty

You can tell from my title that my page includes a list of reasons why girls are fun. I like to liven up my lists, and here I wanted to add a fun twist to the bullet points. Each bullet is actually two brads, a tiny one inserted into a much larger brad. The technique is so simple and yet lends a colorful twist to my list.

Supplies: Patterned paper (CherryArte, Scenic Route); letters (American Crafts, Doodlebug); brads (American Crafts, Heidi Swapp); adhesive (Glue Dots)

materials

large brad	permanent marker
small brad	Crop-A-Dile
ruler	

one

Using a ruler, measure and mark the center point of the larger brad.

two

Open the prongs on the large brad. Then punch a hole in the brad where you made your mark.

three

Insert the smaller brad into the hole.

Recolor and texturize brads

Jamie wanted to dress her pretty pink scallops in a perfect row of brads—but gold just wouldn't do. So she decided to paint her brads pink and soften their texture with flocking powder. The result is a row of brads that perfectly match the sweet theme of her page. It's the happiest layout on earth!

Supplies: Cardstock (Bazzill); patterned paper (Anna Griffin); scalloped paper (Creative Imaginations); brads, paint (Making Memories); flocking (Stampendous); adhesive (Mono Adhesive)

Artwork by Jamie Harper

materials

brad

sanding file or sponge

tweezers

acrylic paint

paper towel

flocking powder (same color as paint)

one

Sand off the color on the brad using a sanding file or sponge.

two

Dip the brad in the paint using tweezers to hold the brad. Gently dab the brad on a paper towel to remove excess paint.

three

Dip the wet brad in the flocking powder. Gently shake the brad to remove excess flock. Allow it to dry.

buttons

Buttons have been used as clothing accessories for centuries. With their popularity, it seems as if they have also been used as accessories for our scrapbook pages for just as long. Because of their versatility and variety of sizes, shapes and color, buttons naturally make for great embellishments. You can stitch buttons to a page, of course, but what happens on a page when we think outside the sewing box? Let's take a look at the ideas in this chapter. You'll see that using buttons on a page will make them cute as a … well, you know.

buttons

Fill holes with puff paint

I have a confession to make: I don't sew. I never find myself sewing a lost button back onto an item of clothing, let alone threading a button for a scrapbook page. While I like the look of filled-up buttonholes, thread is obviously not an option for me. So, I came up with a solution to fill the holes with color without employing a needle and thread. Puff paint comes in small tubes with a fine tip on the end making it easy to fill those holes. The idea is an ace in the hole (or four)!

Supplies: Patterned paper (Luxe Designs, Fancy Pants); brads, eyelets, buttons, bookplate, chipboard (Fancy Pants); letters (Scenic Route, Making Memories); puff paint (Tulip); adhesive (3M, Glue Dots)

materials
sew-through button
puff paint
paper towel or cloth

one

Fill each buttonhole with puff paint.

two

Carefully smooth away any excess paint that seeps out of the holes. Let the puff paint dry.

Supplies: Cardstock (Prism); patterned paper (Cosmo Cricket, Sassafras Lass); chipboard butterflies, buttons and letters (American Crafts); acrylic flowers (Maya Road); buttons (Creative Imaginations); ribbon (May Arts); rhinestones (Doodlebug); die-cut accent (Sassafras Lass)

BE CREATIVE WITH BUTTONS

I love the multiple techniques Melissa employed using buttons to adorn this adorable page about her sweet little daughter. The techniques add an element of fun, and are so easy to duplicate. First, Melissa dressed up the petals of sheer flowers with buttons. She stacked two buttons to make the centers pop. She also crisscrossed playful gingham ribbon through the holes of button-shaped chipboard, letting the ends peek out underneath. Finally, she tied a pretty bow through the holes in another chipboard button to complete the page.

Artwork by Melissa Phillips

PRESS PAINT INTO HOLES

Suzy opted to try a variation on the puff paint idea featured on my "M & EM" layout on the opposite page. She pooled acrylic paint on her background, then pressed her buttons into the pools, using the paint as adhesive. This action forced the paint up into the holes of the button. What a fabulous border for Suzy's page about the close relationship she has with her daughter.

Supplies: Patterned paper, stickers (Adornit); chipboard letters (Heidi Swapp); buttons (Autumn Leaves, unknown); flowers (Sweetwater); adhesive (Aleene's); Misc: paint

Artwork by Suzy Plantamura

2 HANDBOOK HOW-TO | KICK IT UP

Accessorize buttons with rub-ons

When Madison arranged her shrimp around

this bowl, it looked almost as good as...

I loved the idea of using buttons to pump up this page. But the plain black buttons I had needed some color to make them pop. Rub-ons turned out to be a quick and easy way to dress up the buttons. The burst of red on each button reminds me of the cocktail sauce in the center of the circle of shrimp my daughter so lovingly arranged. Just the right detail for this page.

Supplies: Cardstock (Bazzill); patterned paper (Paper Trunk, Reminisce); letter stickers (Arctic Frog, Making Memories); chipboard (Rusty Pickle); brads, buttons, eyelets (American Crafts); ribbon (Making Memories); rub-ons (Heidi Grace); adhesive (3M, Glue Dots)

materials
button
rub-on
micro-tip scissors
craft stick or stylus

one

Cut out the rub-on image using micro-tip scissors. Make sure the rub-on does not extend beyond the edges of the button.

two

Rub on the image to the top of the button using a stylus or craft stick, making sure the edges along the perimeter of the button are attached fully.

TAKE BUTTONS TO ANOTHER DIMENSION

While Melissa embellished her flowers with buttons (on page 27), Kimber used buttons as her flower embellishments. Using buttons attached to curled-up wire mimics the flowers in the garden and adds playful dimension to the page. Layering smaller buttons on top of a larger ones gives the flowers even more dimension. These embellishments, which command attention, make it easy to see that this page is all about a special garden Kimber's son and his grandmother planted.

Supplies: Cardstock (WorldWin); patterned paper (My Mind's Eye); letter stickers (Arctic Frog); chipboard accents (Sandylion); buttons (Autumn Leaves); Misc: wire

Artwork by Kimber McGray

"SEA" HOW BUTTONS ENHANCE A THEME

Did you know that centuries ago some buttons were made of seashells? It's fitting, then, that I used buttons to mimic the seashells found at the ocean. Embedding these buttons in modeling paste "sand" translates the feeling of being by the sea. The mixture of modeling paste and mesh holds the buttons in place and provides an anchor for my frothy photo. The image of my daughter enjoying a wave in the ocean captures the essence of our time at the beach perfectly. So I'm thrilled with how well these embellishments reinforce that theme.

Supplies: Cardstock (Bazzill); patterned paper, stickers (Creative Imaginations); brads, buttons, eyelets (Autumn Leaves); modeling paste (Jo Sonja's Crackle Paste); adhesive (3M, Glue Dots); Misc: mesh

String beads on buttons

buttons

The creative ideas that Judi comes up with usually leave me speechless, and this button technique is no exception. The beaded wire adds texture and shine to these flower centers, perfect for the theme of the layout. It makes you want to reach out and touch the page! For your own layout, you can use a variety of bead types and sizes. You can also follow Judi's lead and string beaded leaves to match your flowers.

Artwork by Judi VanValkinburg

Supplies: Cardstock (Bazzill); patterned paper (Making Memories, My Mind's Eye); chipboard letters (American Crafts); buttons (Autumn Leaves); paper trim (Doodlebug); flowers (Making Memories); sticker (7gypsies); beads (Walmart); adhesive (Glue Dots, Tombow); Misc: floral wire

QUICK TIP

Adhesive dots are the quickest way to attach buttons, and they make for a strong bond.

materials

sew-through buttons   adhesive dot

wire (24-gauge)   silk or paper flower

beads (at least 16)

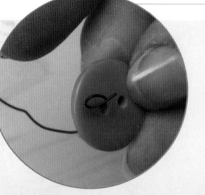

one

Create a loop at one end of the wire and thread through a buttonhole.

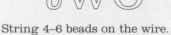

two

String 4–6 beads on the wire.

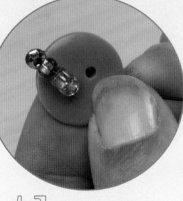

three

Wrap the beaded wire around the button's edge to the back. Then thread the wire through the next hole to the front. Repeat steps 2–3 with four more beads. Continue stringing beads until you are satisfied with the look of the button.

four

After you thread the wire through the back for the last time, tie the ends together and trim the excess. Then add an adhesive dot to the back of the button and attach it to the flower.

chipboard

When you think about what chipboard actually is—pressed pieces of plain paper glued together to form a solid piece—its intense popularity as an embellishment seems a little crazy. But it's not chipboard's simplicity that makes it so popular. It is its versatility and alterability, and its dimension helps, too. Finished chipboard easily dresses up a layout, and plain chipboard pieces can be customized with so many mediums, making chipboard work for just about any page. In this section, we'll explore chipboard techniques—chipboard is so versatile we really could devote an entire book to it! Instead, let these ideas spur some of your own.

chipboard

Seeing Jason's face light up whenever Spyke is nearby allows me to over look the messes he makes

or the smells that linger behind. I still draw the line when it comes to the torture he inflicts on my cats

MAN'S
best friend

GO IN CIRCLES

I wanted to create a page using those leftover circles that most of us pop out of our chipboard sheets and throw away. Those circles make a cool graphic border when you simply paint them and line them up in a row. I love the idea of using something I normally would toss to create the finishing touch on this page about my husband and our family dog. The chipboard adds the perfect pop of color around my photos, making a great border for the page.

Supplies: Patterned paper (Chatterbox); chipboard shapes (Fancy Pants); letter stickers (American Crafts, Scenic Route); adhesive (Glue Dots); Misc: paint

MAKE CHIPBOARD SPARKLE AND SHINE

Rita captured the playful spirit of her daughter by covering her chipboard circles with colorful glitter. Most of us grew up using glitter for school projects, so it conjures images of childhood fun. Anyone who sees this page will instantly feel the theme shine right through. Covering the chipboard with a coat of liquid adhesive and liberally applying glitter results in a perfectly shimmery shape.

Supplies: Cardstock (Prism); chipboard shapes (Scenic Route); board clips (Making Memories); glitter (Martha Stewart); glitter chipboard letter and heart (Li'l Davis); letter stickers (Doodlebug); adhesive (Glue Dots); Misc: ribbon

Artwork by Rita Weiss

★I should know better by now

Asking Fletcher to let me take a photograph

of his new haircut would result in this....

Don't tell him that I secretly love this about him★

goof
Ball

You can transform any chipboard shape into an embellishment that matches any layout by covering chipboard with patterned paper. Your options are limited only by the styles of paper in your stash. For this page about my son's goofy spirit, I wanted to match the chipboard frame and star to the background paper. Covering the chipboard allowed me to make that choice, and make a great page.

Supplies: Patterned paper (Paper Trunk); chipboard shapes (Li'l Davis, Rusty Pickle); letters (American Crafts); transparency (Hambly); adhesive (3M, Glue Dots)

materials

raw chipboard

adhesive

patterned paper

craft knife

craft mat

sanding sponge or ink (optional)

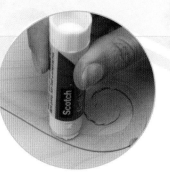

one

Apply adhesive to the top of the chipboard piece.

two

Place the patterned paper with the front facedown. Set the chipboard piece on top of the paper with the adhesive side facedown.

three

Use the craft knife to cut around the piece. Sand or ink the edges, if desired. (This helps hide uneven edges.)

Artwork by Suzy Plantamura

WEAVE PAPER OVER CHIPBOARD

The technique that Suzy used to dress her chipboard tree looks time-consuming and complicated, but looks can be deceiving. She simply took several strips of various patterned papers and wove the strips across the chipboard. Once she had a pattern she was happy with, she applied dimensional gloss medium over the top of the chipboard to seal the papers. The result is an adorable tree—and a technique you can use in a variety of ways.

Supplies: Patterned paper (Anna Griffin, Autumn Leaves, CherryArte, Creative Imaginations, Me & My Big Ideas, MMI, NRN); chipboard letters and shapes (Maya Road); buttons (Autumn Leaves); ribbon (KI Memories); glossy topcoat, paint (Ranger)

MAKE CHIPBOARD "SEW" PRETTY

As I've said before, I don't like to sew. However, Melissa makes me want to reconsider. The textured chipboard details on this page make you linger over this layout, wanting to to soak it all in. She masterfully layered several chipboard shapes together after lightly sanding them for a roughed up, shabby chic look. The sewing is the icing on the cake and provides the perfect amount of texture and detail for this layout about not growing up too fast.

Supplies: Patterned paper (Creative Imaginations, Making Memories, Paper Salon); chipboard glitter flower and letters, tag (Melissa Frances); chipboard flourishes (Jenni Bowlin); chipboard frames and shapes (Making Memories); chipboard strips (Heidi Swapp); rub-on letters (Scenic Route); letter stickers (EK Success); ribbon (American Crafts); button (SEI); Misc: felt

Artwork by Melissa Phillips

Fill space in chipboard

This page captures a significant moment in every married girl's life—The Proposal. To make this page extra special, Judi assembled these gorgeous embellishments using a transparency and cut-out chipboard, filling the empty space with dimensional gloss medium. These fancy, shimmering embellishments have just the right amount of flair for an important layout.

Supplies: Cardstock (Bazzill, Prism); transparency (Hammermill, Luxe); chipboard letters and shapes (BasicGrey, Maya Road); ribbon (Tiffany & Co.); glaze medium (Ranger); adhesive (Duck, Glue Dots, Tombow)

materials

chipboard piece with center cut out

acrylic paint (optional)

adhesive

printed transparency

scissors

dimensional gloss medium

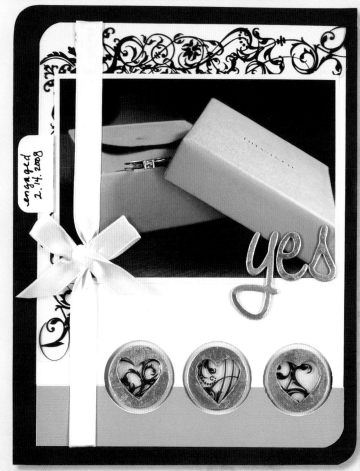

Artwork by Judi VanValkinburg

one

If your chipboard is raw, paint it. Then adhere it to the top of a printed transparency.

two

Trim off the excess transparency around the chipboard piece.

three

Fill the center of the chipboard with dimensional gloss medium, and let it dry overnight.

Artwork by Judi Van Valkinburg

EMBOSS CHIPBOARD SHAPES

As demonstrated in the acrylic section, embossing adds both texture and detail to an embellishment. Embossing these white chipboard shapes resulted in a look that mimics real snowflakes. After Judi embossed her chipboard flakes, she added detailing using seed beads. You get the impression that just like actual snowflakes, no two embossed flakes are exactly alike.

Supplies: Cardstock (Bazzill, Prism); journal accent, patterned paper (Making Memories); letter stickers, paper trim (Doodlebug); chipboard (Maya Road); embossing folder (ProvoCraft); acrylic accents (Heidi Grace); adhesive (3M, Glue Dots, Tombow); software (Sure Cuts A Lot); Misc: beads, paint

QUICK TIP
If you need raw chipboard and have only finished chipboard, sand away the color or peel away the top layer with a craft knife.

Make a photo pop

Artwork by Judi VanValkinburg

Judi came up with this great idea for giving a photo a 3-D effect using chipboard title letters. It's a subtle design technique that really makes the page stand out—and up. You don't have to highlight a cityscape as Judi did. You could use any type of photo with letters of your choice or use various shapes instead. It will make for a unique look for any layout.

Supplies: Cardstock (Bazzill, Prism); transparency (Hambly); chipboard letters and shapes (Making Memories, Maya Road); stickers (7gypsies, American Crafts, K&Co., Making Memories); die-cut accent (QuicKutz); brad (Around the Block); adhesive (Glue Dots, Tombow)

materials

two identical photos

raw chipboard letters

adhesive

craft knife

one

Place the chipboard letters over one of the photos to determine a rough placement of your title on the photo.

two

Add adhesive to the front of the letters. Set them facedown on the back of a photo. Place the letters in the spot where you want your title to appear (as determined in step 1).

three

Cut out the letters using a craft knife.

four

Adhere the letters to the top of the other photo. Carefully place each letter over its identical portion of the photo.

die-cuts

Die-cuts go back to the early years of scrapbooking. Remember the days of adding a die-cut pumpkin, sun, basketball, or whatever else matched your layout's theme? Fortunately, this old-school scrapbook staple has evolved along with the craft and continues to find a place on our layouts. Essentially, a die-cut is heavy-weight paper that has been precut to a shape. One of the great things about modern die-cuts is that often manufacturers offer a line of die-cuts that coordinates with a collection of papers, which takes the guesswork out of choosing what die-cuts to use. The downside of die-cuts is their lack of any dimension. So it begs the question, "How do I breathe new life into a flat die-cut?" Turn the page to find the answers.

Distress floral die-cuts

die-cuts

Artwork by Rita Weiss

What could be more fitting for a page about a daughter's love for flowers than a bouquet of die-cut floral shapes? Rita took her die-cut flowers from flat to fabulous by distressing them. Easy peasy! The alteration gives the flowers a lift, and ups their visual interest. You can do the same on a layout, employing one distressing method or all three! The result will transform ordinary die-cuts into a floral showcase.

Supplies: Cardstock (Prism); die-cut shapes, patterned paper (BasicGrey); rub-ons (Prima); chipboard letters (American Crafts); adhesive (Glue Dots, Making Memories)

materials
flower die-cuts

inkpad

one
Ink the edges of the die-cut.

two
Bend the edges of the petals upward.

three
Tear the edges of the die-cut and fold them up a bit.

Supplies: Cardstock (Bazzill); patterned paper (BasicGrey, Jenni Bowlin, Making Memories); die-cuts (Jenni Bowlin, Scenic Route); chipboard frame (Scenic Route); letter stickers (American Crafts); flowers, trim (Prima); brads (Making Memories); bird accent (Autumn Leaves)

BUILD ON A DIE-CUT FOUNDATION

Instead of altering her die-cuts, Melissa simply built upon them. The various die-cut journaling blocks act as a mat for the title letters. The variety of shapes and styles inspires a playful feel and makes a simple title eye-catching. Layering is the key to pulling off this look, and the sweet ribbon bows tie it together nicely. Melissa's innovative use of journaling die-cuts illustrates that die-cuts can be used in ways other than their intended purpose.

Artwork by Melissa Phillips

PUNCH YOUR OWN DIE-CUTS

When you punch a shape from patterned paper, you've essentially created your own die-cut. Jamie's example demonstrates a simple way to use handmade die-cuts. The theme of this page is patchwork quilts, and Jamie placed a variety of stars punched from patterned paper in rows to mimic the look of a quilt. The paper patchwork evokes a feeling of warmth and love, which echoes the words Jamie wrote about her love for her children.

Supplies: Cardstock (Bazzill); patterned paper (Dreamstreet); star paper punch (Fiskars); rubons (Scenic Route); rhinestones (Me & My Big Ideas); buttons (Autumn Leaves)

Artwork by Jamie Harper

2 HANDBOOK HOW-TO | KICK IT UP
Make die-cuts clearly shine

I challenged myself to integrate several die-cuts into the design of this page. I ended up lining them around the perimeter of the layout. Not content to leave the die-cuts alone, I added a dash of pizzazz with printed transparencies and a sprinkling of glitter. Even though the journaling has a serious tone, I wanted the page to reflect the hopeful nature I was feeling about my son. The sparkling border frames my photo nicely and allows it to take center stage.

Supplies: Cardstock (Bazzill); die-cuts, letter stickers (BasicGrey); transparency (Hambly); adhesive (3M, Glue Dots)

QUICK TIP
Die-cutting machines can cut more than just paper. Consider the possibilities in die-cut fabric, transparencies, felt and more!

materials

die-cut frame	micro-tip scissors
adhesive	spray adhesive
printed transparency	glitter

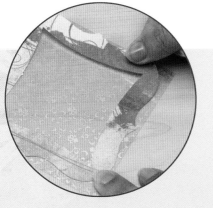

one

Apply adhesive to the back of the die-cut. Then place the die-cut face up over the top of the transparency.

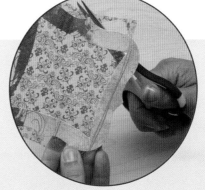

two

Cut off the excess transparency using micro-tip scissors.

three

Coat the back of the transparency with spray adhesive.

four

Sprinkle glitter over the adhesive.

INVEST IN A DIE-CUTTING MACHINE

A die-cutting machine helped Judi layer glittery cardstock and felt to construct a spectacular card. A variety of die-cutting machines can help you achieve this look. Judi used the Quickutz and Cuttlebug machines to create the die-cuts on the card. Also, she illustrates that die-cuts don't always have to be made of paper. She used a variety of materials to provide texture and playfulness. This card's recipient will surely be thrilled.

Artwork by Judi VanValkinburg

Supplies: Cardstock (Bazzill, Prism); patterned paper (KI Memories); glitter cardstock (Doodlebug); die-cutters (Provo Craft, QuicKutz); embossing folder (Provo Craft); stamp (Inque Boutique); felt (Stick-It Felt); brad (K&Co.); adhesive (3M, Glue Dots, Tombow)

DRESS UP A DIE-CUT

Cindy practically threw the kitchen sink at these die-cut butterflies! She used glitter paint, stitching around the edges, French knots and buttons. Don't be afraid to dress up a die-cut. Think of it like a little black dress that you can accessorize. In this case, Cindy dressed her die-cuts to the nines.

Supplies: Cardstock (Prism); die-cuts, patterned paper, ribbon, rub-ons (Fancy Pants); chipboard shapes (Fancy Pants, Jenni Bowlin); buttons (My Mind's Eye); paper trim (Doodlebug); tag (Martha Stewart); glitter paint (DecoArt); adhesive (Glue Dots, Kokuyo); Misc: floss

Artwork by Cindy Tobey

Make die-cuts crackle & pop

Perhaps you can relate to my family situation: I have one child who moves like a turtle in the morning and another who I can't slow down long enough to eat a decent breakfast. The old Brothers Grimm fable about the tortoise and the hare came to mind, so I wanted the embellishments to have a fairy tale feel. Ranger's Crackle Accents gives the die-cuts an aged look and coiled wire supplies some extra dimension.

Supplies: Die-cuts, patterned paper (BasicGrey); letter stickers (American Crafts, BasicGrey, Jenni Bowlin); crackle paint (Ranger); adhesive (Glue Dots); Misc: wire

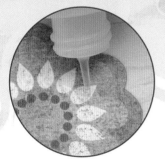

one

Apply a layer of the dimensional crackle medium to the die-cut. You can outline particular elements or coat the entire shape. Allow the crackle medium to dry and watch the crackle appear.

two

Wrap wire around a pencil or pen about eight times (depending on how long you want your coil to be). Remove the wire from the pencil.

three

Attach a thick adhesive dot to the back of your die-cut, and embed the end of the coiled wire into the dot. Attach the other end of the wire to the background of your page using the same method.

materials

die-cut shape

dimensional crackle medium
(like Crackle Accents)

pen or pencil

wire (24-guage)

thick adhesive dots

digital

A relatively new category that is gaining attention, digital embellishments truly are the most customizable embellishments you can find. Not only can you change the color, you can change the size, alter the shape, flip the orientation, and then print as many as you need and alter them even more. The only limit is your imagination—and your access to a computer. But don't think digital means difficult. These embellishments are easy to use. Visit digital scrapbooking Web sites (like www.designerdigitals.com and www.shabbyprincess.com) to find a wide array of designs and styles to suit your needs. Before you know it, you'll have your own little digi stash to use and reuse.

LAYER A DIGI TITLE

I love to layer my clothes (the better to hide the flaws, my dear), and I love to layer my embellishments, too. On this layout, I layered digi designs with title letters. I changed the size of the digital flower embellishments and added colors to match my layout. Then I layered several different flowers on top of one another. The result is an embellished title that perfectly matches the color scheme on this page.

Supplies: Epoxy sticker, journaling tag, patterned paper (Luxe); rub-ons (Daisy D's, Luxe); digital elements by Katie Pertiet, Anna Aspnes and MaryAnn Wise (Designer Digitals)

PRINT EMBELLISHMENTS ON BACKGROUNDS

Cindy used digital paint-spattered star embellishments to liven up her page. Printing the simple stars directly on the background paper provides an unexpected look. To make the stars shine, she stitched the edges. Cindy used the same technique to create her star-shaped journaling block. Together, all the elements make this layout design a bright idea.

Supplies: Cardstock (WorldWin); arrow accent, patterned paper, ribbon (Prima); letter stickers (American Crafts); brads (Queen & Co.); buttons (Autumn Leaves, My Mind's Eye); digital elements by Kim Christensen (Prima Hybrid)

Artwork by Cindy Tobey

Pop up digital elements

Do you ever wonder what your pet is dreaming? Janet pondered that very question on this page about her sweet kitty. She embellished this page with various types of digital birds that she printed, cut out and mounted on pop dots. Creating her own digital die-cuts allowed her to print as many as she needed and in various sizes. Popping them off the page breathes life into her design.

Artwork by Janet Ohlson

Supplies: Cardstock (WorldWin); patterned paper (Scenic Route); flowers (American Crafts); letter stickers (American Crafts, Doodlebug); brads (Junkitz); digital bird stamps by Lynn Grieveson (Designer Digitals)

materials

Adobe Photoshop Elements

digital embellishments

white cardstock

printer

micro-tip scissors

adhesive foam

one

Place all the digital embellishments in an 8.5" × 11" (22cm × 28cm) document in Photoshop (File>New). Resize them as needed. Print the file onto white cardstock.

two

Cut out each image using micro-tip scissors. Add adhesive foam to the back of the embellishments before placing them on your layout.

2 HANDBOOK HOW-TO | KICK IT UP
Fashion faux epoxy stickers

Artwork by Suzy Plantamura

Suzy's daughter makes her laugh, and Suzy's page makes me smile. I love the playfulness of her embellishments, the colors she chose and the pops of shiny patterns. To create her own embellishments, she printed digital borders and circles onto white cardstock and cut them out. She accented the printed border with tiny brads and turned the printed circles into homemade epoxy accents that fit the page perfectly.

Supplies: Cardstock (Bazzill, WorldWin); chipboard letters (Me & My Big Ideas); brads (Junkitz, Queen & Co., other); digital elements by Katie Pertiet (Designer Digitals); Misc: markers

QUICK TIP
Changing the color of any digital embellishment is easy using Photoshop Elements. Go to Enhance>Adjust Color>Adjust Hue/Saturation. Adjust the sliders as needed to change the different colors. To change the whole embellishment to a single color, click on Colorize.

one

Print the digital embellishments onto cardstock. Then cut them out.

two

Adhere printed embellishments to a sheet of chipboard. Cut out the embellishments.

three

Coat the embellishments generously with dimensional gloss medium (at least two layers).

four

Allow the dimensional gloss medium to dry (about four hours). Add adhesive foam to the back of an embellishment before attaching it to the layout.

Artwork by Kimber McGray

FLIP OVER DIGI EMBELLISHMENTS

Another reason digital embellishments are so versatile is that you can easily flip the image (so that it faces the reverse of its original direction). This allows you to use the embellishment however you need on your page. On Kimber's page, one of these adorable squirrels just wasn't enough to highlight the cute journaling. Placing two facing squirrels gives the words more emphasis and reinforces the theme as well.

Supplies: Cardstock (WorldWin); patterned paper (Making Memories, We R Memory Keepers); chipboard letters (American Crafts); letter stickers (Doodlebug); chipboard accents (We R Memory Keepers); digital elements by Andrea Victoria (Designer Digitals)

FAKE THE LOOK OF 3-D EMBELLISHMENTS

Check out this 3-D flourish that Janet crafted for this page about her dressed up son. While this technique requires a little time and patience, it is actually pretty easy to complete. Janet started by printing her embellishment twice—once onto cardstock and once onto patterned paper. Then she cut both out and layered them on her page, using adhesive foam to make the top layer pop. Notice that she also staggered the placement to produce a shadowing effect. It's a cool technique—just imagine all the ways you can adapt it.

Supplies: Cardstock (WorldWin); letter stickers, patterned paper (American Crafts); brads (Junkitz); digital brush by Anna Aspnes (Designer Digitals)

Artwork by Janet Ohlson

Transfer your own rub-on designs

I adore rub-ons and I'm always on the lookout for great designs. I used to cringe when I saw digital brushes and embellishment designs that would have been perfect had they been rub-ons. No more cringing! I discovered rub-on transfer paper and tried transferring a digital image using this paper. The technique worked wonderfully and also provided an additional printed embellishment (the leftover transparency) to use on the page.

Supplies: Cardstock (Prism); patterned paper (7gypsies, My Mind's Eye, Prima); letter stickers (Making Memories); transparency (Printworks); rub-on transfer paper (EK Success); adhesive (Glue Dots); Misc: rhinestones

materials

digital design
transparency sheet
printer
run-on transfer paper
stylus or ballpoint pen

one

Print the digital image onto a transparency. Set the rub-on transfer paper (with the rub-on side facedown) on your background. Set the transparency on top of the transfer paper.

two

Trace over the digital image using a stylus or ballpoint pen.

three

Lift the transfer paper periodically to check the transfer. Cut out the leftover transparency image.

eyelets

There was a time when eyelets were most commonly seen on shoes or belts. But scrapbookers are known for their resourcefulness and eventually took it upon themselves to utilize eyelets in various places on their projects, making them a hot commodity. What makes eyelets so useful is their ability to keep two items together, but their holes allow for looping fibers or simply creating unique designs. Like a good scrapbooker, you likely scooped up many eyelets in many sizes and colors when they were all the rage. No worries! If you're left with an overabundance of eyelets and only a few ideas, this section is for you.

1

HANDBOOK HOW-TO | SIMPLY CREATE
Adorn flowers with large eyelets

Artwork by Melissa Phillips

After I soaked in the sweetness of Melissa's layout, I thought, super simple and yet so very pretty! I often add brads to flowers, but never thought to add eyelets. Large eyelets that spell a special word or hold an embossed design offer the perfect adornment for fabric flowers. Melissa tucked her dressed up flowers into a bookplate, framing them on the page.

Supplies: Patterned paper (BasicGrey, Melissa Frances); eyelets (We R Memory Keepers); bookplate, letter and shape stickers (BasicGrey); chipboard letters (American Crafts); buttons (Melissa Frances); ribbon (Martha Stewart); hemp (Stampin' Up); pinking shears (Fiskars); Misc: flowers

materials
fabric flower
large decorative eyelet
Crop-A-Dile

one

Punch a hole in the center of the flower using the Crop-A-Dile.

two

Place the eyelets in the flower's hole.

three

Set the eyelet using the Crop-A-Dile.

FASTEN TRANSPARENCIES WITH EYELETS

Transparencies make great additions to layouts, but attaching them can be tricky. Any attempt at using adhesive will show right through. Eyelets offer an excellent solution. On this page, I layered several printed transparencies, using small silver eyelets to hold them in place. The eyelets not only provide seamless adhesion, but add to the design as well.

Supplies: Patterned paper, transparency (Creative Imaginations, Hambly); eyelets (American Crafts); decorative tape (7gypsies); photo corner (Making Memories); tags (Office Depot); adhesive (Glue Dots)

SUBSTITUTE EYELETS FOR CIRCULAR SHAPES

Anyone that knows a child under 14 has probably encountered a Webkinz. These soft, furry stuffed animals have taken over my home, and I couldn't resist building a page to document their significance to our family. Using eyelets to mimic the eyes of the paper pieced Webkinz brings the animals to life. Consider using eyelets in place of a number a circular objects, such as dots on a ladybug, buttons on a dress, bubbles in a bath and stars in a night sky.

Supplies: Cardstock (Prism); patterned paper, rub-ons (Luxe); eyelets (American Crafts); letter stickers (EK Success, Luxe, Making Memories); adhesive (Glue Dots)

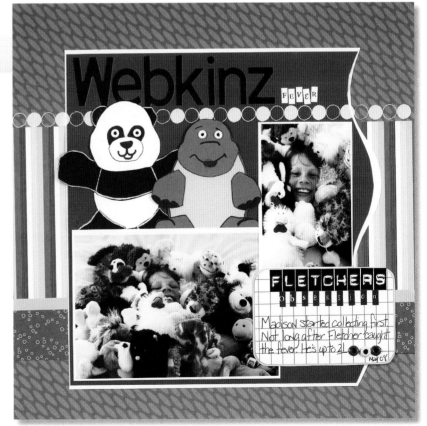

eyelets

Dressing up plain chipboard is as easy as grabbing a Crop-A-Dile and a pile of eyelets. Judi's card packs a huge punch of color with her assortment of eyelets scattered throughout the letters. She even tied her ribbon through an eyelet placed in the greeting tag. Any small eyelets work well for this technique and allow you to make a dent in a large stash.

Supplies: Cardstock (Bazzill, Prism); eyelets (Making Memories); chipboard letters (Maya Road); die-cut (Provo Craft); ribbons (Offray, unknown); adhesive (Duck)

Artwork by Melissa Phillips

materials
chipboard letter
Crop-A-Dile
assortment of eyelets

Punch holes in the letter.

Set eyelets in the holes.

QUICK TIP
Using a Crop-A-Dile to set eyelets is no doubt the easiest way to get the job done. To set eyelets correctly using the Crop-A-Dile, insert one of the "pointy" ends through the hole in the top of the eyelet.

Craft an eyelet vine

Rita illustrates another fabulous idea that requires plenty of eyelets. Prior to punching, she drew the design of a vine in the center of the page and randomly set the eyelets along the vine. She also attached flowers and photos in various spots on the vine using eyelets to hold them in place. You can draw other designs—like simple loops, swirls or circles—to pull off a similar look, which is what makes this technique versatile.

Supplies: Cardstock (WorldWin); eyelets (American Crafts); chipboard letters, flowers (Prima); adhesive (Making Memories)

Artwork by Rita Weiss

materials
pencil

hole punch

assortment of eyelets

eyelet setter or Crop-A-Dile

one

Sketch a vine shape that winds through the center of your background.

two

Randomly place holes throughout the vine. I placed mine about 1" (3cm) apart, but you can make yours closer if you like.

three

Add eyelets to the holes. Attach flowers in spots along the vine. Trace over the pencil lines in pen or erase them.

fabric

Taking after eyelets and buttons, fabric naturally transitions from the sewing table to the scrapbook page as well. Like paper, fabric offers a variety of patterns and colors, but fabric is also flexible and provides a textile experience. Beyond those fabulous attributes, fabric is found virtually everywhere. Clothing children have outgrown, remnants from sewing projects, vintage bedding and curtains are just some of the various places you can find fabric to transform a layout. Fabric lines specifically designed for scrapbookers are gaining popularity as well. Not just for the quilting circle anymore, fabric is a wonderful embellishment for clothing your scrapbook pages in style.

Little Miss Personality! 03-08

Whenever I try to take pictures of Chloe, she just makes silly faces. It's almost impossible to get a good picture of her!

GENERATE WARMTH

Artwork by Suzy Plantamura

This page has a quilt-like feel with warm, homespun charm. Suzy could have used patterned paper to fashion a similar look, but using fabric with frayed edges conveys the message of love and warmth better than paper. The buttons, rickrack and crochet pieces reinforce the message as well, along with the stitching that frames the page. Altogether, the elements make me want to cozy up to the layout.

Supplies: Cardstock (Prism); fabric (Jo-Ann's); rickrack (Making Memories, unknown); buttons (Autumn Leaves, unknown); crochet butterfly (Maya Road); Misc: chipboard letters, markers, thread

1

Alter fabric flowers

For this layout, I altered the color of some crochet flowers with fabric paints and glitter to better suit the colors in my page. I wanted to use these flowers because they went perfectly with the flowers on my daughter's hat in her photos, but the original bright green hue was a bit much for the page. The solution was to paint them blue and when they were dry, add them to my page. Problem solved!

materials

fabric flower
fabric paint
sponge brush
glitter glue

Supplies: Cardstock (Prism); patterned paper (Daisy D's, Prima); fabric flowers (Imaginisce); transparency (Hambly); letters (Doodlebug, Making Memories); paint (Heidi Swapp); glitter (Making Memories); adhesive (3M, Glue Dots)

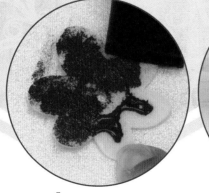

one

Apply paint to the flower.

two

Brush the paint until the entire flower is covered.

three

Add glitter glue to the flower and allow it to dry.

sweet baby

cakes

sweet Sierra on her 1st birthday.

SWEETEN A PAGE WITH FABRIC SCRAPS

Artwork by Melissa Phillips

Melissa's textured creations never cease to surprise me. Her creative use of fabric is a sweet addition to this page all about ... sweets, of course! Using fabric for the tops of the cupcakes provides texture and dimension. And they're simple to make: Just cut a circle out of a fabric scrap (Melissa used flannel for extra texture), fold it in half and stitch the halves together.

Supplies: Cardstock (WorldWin); patterned paper (BasicGrey, Cosmo Cricket, Making Memories); fabric (craft store); chipboard letters (Prima); flowers, glitter brads (Making Memories); sticker accents (BasicGrey, Cosmo Cricket); buttons, trim (Melissa Frances); twill tape (Wright's)

Cover chipboard with fabric

What could be more fitting for a page about worn-out jeans than worn denim? Here, Kimber opted to cover her chipboard title letters with fabric. She frayed the edges of the material a bit to enhance the worn feel. Just a glance at the words gives you an immediate sense of the page's theme. This technique works well for many page topics just by changing the fabric you use.

Supplies: Cardstock (WorldWin); letter stickers (American Crafts); chipboard letters (BasicGrey); denim fabric (unknown); adhesive (Delta)

Artwork by Kimber McGray

materials

chipboard letters

fabric glue

fabric

sharp micro-tip scissors

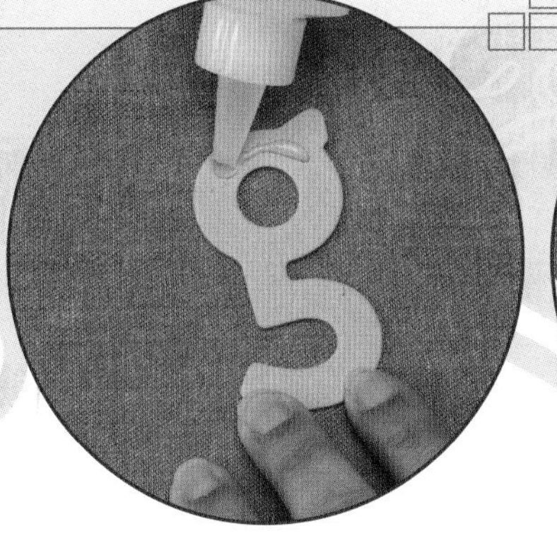

one

Add glue to the top of the letters.

two

Place letters facedown on the wrong side of the fabric.

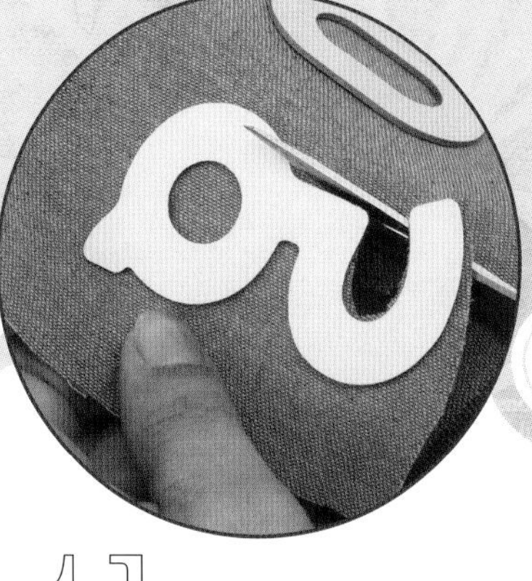

three

Cut out the letters using the scissors.

f a b r i c

3 HANDBOOK HOW-TO | THINK OUTSIDE THE BOX
Fold a fabric ruffle

You can't help but giggle at this cute title. The fabric dots and ruffle treatment underneath lend a happy, playful feel to the layout about Rita's little girl. I bet you are smiling right now just looking at this page. Rita couldn't have done a better job matching the page's theme with her creative fabric embellishments.

Artwork by Rita Weiss

Supplies: Cardstock (Prism); fabric (Michaels); floss (DMC); letter stickers (American Crafts); chipboard letters (Scenic Route)

m a t e r i a l s
fabric

sharp scissors

adhesive dots or fabric glue

floss

needle

 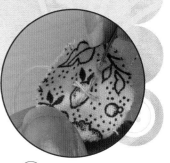

one
Cut your fabric to about twice the size you want the final length and width to be. Then fold the piece of fabric in half lengthwise.

two
Pleat the fabric, folding over sections that are about 1" (3cm). Hold the pleats together using fabric glue or adhesive dots.

three
If desired, add a running stitch to the fabric ruffle using floss.

four
To create circle embellishments, cut a circle about ¾" (2cm) wide from the fabric. Then create a cross-stitch using floss.

As we get older, it can be easy to let your birthday come and go without a lot of fan fare. It tends not to be as big of a deal the older you get. That may be true but this year was actually a little bit more special for Jacob. It was his GOLDEN birthday. The date of his birthday matched the age he was turning. So on May 17th he turned 17 years old and I wanted to make his day extra special. He got a new Ipod that he had been wanting, some cash in his pocket and we went out to dinner at a the Little Dipper where the specialty is fondue dipping. We had a blast and the Party was definitely on!   2008

Party ON

PIECE SWEET SHAPES WITH FABRIC

Do you remember Melissa's cute fabric cupcakes on page 66? It didn't take me long to think of something even more fun to piece together with fabric—an entire cake! It scores extra marks for the felt candles used on top. To make piecing the cake easy, first draw the shape on paper and cut it out in pieces. Then trace the pieces onto fabric and cut those pieces out. For this page, I used stiff, scrapbook-friendly fabric, which is easier to cut and manipulate than traditional fabric. The technique is a piece of cake!

Supplies: Cardstock (Prism); patterned paper (Luxe); fabric paper (KI Memories); fabric (unknown); brads, felt (American Crafts); sequins (Michaels); letter stickers (Doodlebug); paint (Making Memories)

QUICK TIP

If you're cutting shapes from fabric, brush some fabric stiffener onto the fabric (and let it dry) prior to cutting. That will make the task much easier.

fibers

Just as buttons and fabric have crossed
over from the sewing world to paper crafts,
fibers have made the transition from
knitting and embroidery to scrapbooking.
Fibers—particular yarn but also thread
and floss—add soft texture and unique
dimension. When fibers started to make
their way into the scrapbooking aisle,
I began collecting yards and yards of
different colors and textures. It fascinated
me to explore the tactile experience of this
particular embellishment, and I continue to
challenge myself to find interesting ways
to incorporate fibers onto my pages. In this
chapter, you will find incredible examples
that will send you running to the nearest
craft store in search of fabulous fibers.

1 HANDBOOK HOW-TO | SIMPLY CREATE
Frame photos with fibers

I feel so blessed that we live so close to the ocean ... So many photo opportunities... Here are the

best of **Summer** 2007

The colors and texture of the fibers on this layout are reminiscent of frothy ocean waves. So using them as simple picture frames perfectly highlights the summertime photos and provides all the embellishment the page needs. The pop of color against the neutral cardstock background also draws attention to the photos. I wrapped additional fibers around several title letters to tie the design together.

materials
2–3 strands of fiber
adhesive
photos

Supplies: Cardstock (Bazzill); fibers, ribbons (unknown); letter stickers (KI Memories); chipboard letters (Prima); adhesive (3M, Glue Dots)

one
Twist several fibers together to create a custom color. You can twist the fibers loosely or tightly as desired.

two
Apply adhesive (I prefer Glue Lines for this project) around the perimeter of the photos.

three
Apply twisted fibers to the adhesive, making sure the ends are tacked down.

QUICK TIP
Keep adhesive lines on hand when working with fibers. The easy-to-work-with dry adhesive adheres fibers well and eliminates the mess of liquid glue.

Artwork by Rita Weiss

COVER THE BACKGROUND

Rita covered her background with fibers creating a dimensional foundation for her page elements. The fibers' rich texture contrasts with the smooth photos and also provides a bit of the unexpected. Using liquid glue or adhesive lines to attach fibers makes it easy to pull off this technique. It's a great way to use up a fiber stash as big as mine!

Supplies: Cardstock (WorldWin); fibers (BasicGrey); letter stickers (American Crafts); sticker accent (Cloud 9); glitter heart (Melissa Frances); adhesive (Glue Dots, Making Memories)

Artwork by Jamie Harper

WRAP FIBERS AROUND CHIPBOARD

With just a simple twist, Jamie used thin fibers to turn her chipboard flowers into standouts. The contrast of fibers—messy, fluffy fibers and smooth embroidery floss—adds interest to the page. The fiber wrapping on these flowers resembles a Spirograph, which was loads of fun to play with as a child. The image is perfect for a page about these two young girls. You get a feel of childlike joy.

Supplies: Cardstock (Bazzill); chipboard title, patterned paper, sticker accents (Me & My Big Ideas); fibers (BasicGrey); floss (JoAnn Stores); border stamp, chipboard accents (Technique Tuesday); buttons (Scenic Route)

The fibers in Suzy's splashing waves and shining sun bring this page to life. You can almost hear the ocean breeze blowing and the sound of waves crashing on the shore when you look at this layout. With the right fiber colors, you can highlight any shape your heart desires. All you need is a little adhesive.

Supplies: Cardstock (WorldWin); patterned paper (Adornit, Autumn Leaves); fibers (BasicGrey, unknown); chipboard letters (Maya Road); paint (Delta, Making Memories); adhesive (Aleene's)

catchin' waves

WheN we were iN Hawaii, Sophie waNted to take surfing lessons. I was so worried she was too young until I saw her catchin' waves. She was a Natural and made it look so easy! I was so proud of my little girl!

Kauai
Aug.'07

Artwork by Suzy Plantamura

materials
patterned paper
scissors
adhesive
fiber

one
Cut a shape from patterned paper. Apply swirls of adhesive to it. I made a spiral, but you might try curves or stripes instead.

two
Apply fiber to the adhesive. Allow wet adhesive to dry.

Loop fiber around a page

Artwork by Cindy Tobey

Cindy came up with the most suitable embellishment for this page about her favorite winter hobby. Looping yarn in and out of eyelets is a fitting way to enhance a knitting-themed layout. The technique can be used with any kind of fiber. Try smooth elastic fiber for a modern design, or thick, velvety fiber for a more traditional layout.

Supplies: Cardstock (Bazzill); chipboard letters, eyelets, patterned paper, ribbon (We R Memory Keepers); yarn (Briar Rose Fibers); knitting needle (Clover); letter stickers, paint (Making Memories); flower (Queen & Co.); buttons (Autumn Leaves); adhesive (Glue Dots, Kokuyo)

materials

cardstock or photo

eyelets

eyelet setter or Crop-A-Dile

long strand of fiber

stylus (optional)

tape

one

Set eyelets in various locations along the edge of the cardstock or photo.

two

Pull the fiber through the first eyelet, using a stylus as needed.

three

Loop the fiber through the remaining eyelets. Tape the fiber ends to the back.

flowers

Unlike brads, fibers, buttons and acrylic, flowers are undoubtedly feminine. But adding flowers to scrapbook pages doesn't always have to dictate a fancy, frilly and formal layout. Using flowers in unique ways can embellish layouts that are fresh and clean, eclectic and playful. And though you find yourself with jars and jars of little paper flowers, there's a limit to the number of times you can scatter them around your page. In this section, the flower embellishment is reinvented—from soft and simple to sweet and cozy to sparkly and jazzy. Come on! Let's get some flower power for your pages.

1

Attach a petal border

To complement the beautiful collage of photos, Suzy deconstructed her flowers to create a simple and unique border of petals. A few different colors create a pattern that matches the colors of her daughter's dress. The petals add texture and dimension to the page while placing them in a wavy line creates movement.

Artwork by Suzy Plantamura

materials

large silk or paper flower

scissors

adhesive

ribbon

my beautiful belle

Chloe got a Belle doll from Grandma Donna and a Belle costume from Grandma Claudia for Christmas. She wore it to Taylor's birthday party. Feb.'08

Supplies: Cardstock (Bazzill, Prism); flowers (Bazzill, Heidi Swapp, Martha Stewart, Prima, unknown); trim (Melissa Frances); chipboard letters used as outline (BasicGrey)

one

Cut off the petals of your flowers.

two

Add a line of adhesive to your background. Then attach the petals in a row along the adhesive line.

three

Place the ribbon on top the petals' ends to hide them.

A gorgeous picture of three kids, all having their birthdays within 6 weeks of each other. They each turn one year older as we greet the summer each year. This has its drawbacks, birthday 'season' is over fairly quick, by the time Abby's birthday rolls around we are all caked out... if there is such a thing. It's hard to spoil each child with a daytrip out, Abby and Jacob's birthdays fall so close together they need turns at a special treat day. This year Abby went to Butterfly Creek on her day. There are some good things about close birthdays though. Like the fact that none of the kids get jealous of the other, because they know that their birthdays are not far away. And the fact that they all start school on the first day of the first term. And then there is the cake. Did I mention the cake?

Artwork by Nic Howard

GATHER A FLORAL BOUQUET

For this layout, Nic gathered several different kinds of flowers—silk, acrylic, paper, felt and epoxy—in several sizes to layer on the page. The result is a flower bouquet that lends an eclectic, more casual feel than silk flowers could alone. The contrast also serves to enhance the individual flower, and none of them fade into the background. Stacking flowers and folding one in half gives the page depth.

Supplies: Patterned paper (Cosmo Cricket, Creative Imaginations, Me & My Big Ideas); transparency (Hambly); paper punch (Fiskars); flowers (unknown); adhesive (Glue Dots)

Fill chipboard with flower confetti

flowers

The empty space in these plain chipboard flowers called out for something more, so I came up with the idea to fill them with—what else?—flowers. I cut up silk and paper flower petals into confetti-like pieces, perfect for a happy-go-lucky page about my daughter and her friend. Several layers of liquid glue hold the pieces in place and allow random pieces to stick up to provide a 3-D effect.

Supplies: Cardstock (Prism); fabric paper (Michael Miller); chipboard flowers (Everlasting Keepsakes, Fancy Pants); flowers (Heidi Swapp, Prima); chipboard letters (BasicGrey); glitter (Making Memories); glossy topcoat (Ranger); Misc: paint

materials

various silk and paper flowers

scissors

chipboard piece with negative space

dimensional gloss medium

one

Cut up the flowers into small pieces.

two

Set the chipboard piece on your background. Fill the space in the chipboard with flower pieces. Then drizzle dimensional gloss medium over the petals.

three

Press the petals to adhere them. Repeat with more dimensional gloss medium as needed to adhere all pieces.

Artwork by Rita Weiss

PAINT FLOWERS A NEW HUE

Consider this solution for flowers that are the wrong color for your project. Painting your flowers the perfect shade to match your page is as simple as a stroke of paint across the petals. Even if you do like the flowers' original hue, a gentle stroke of paint in a color slightly darker than your flower will create shading, adding depth. Rita painted her flowers to coordinate with her patterned paper and highlight her photos.

Supplies: Cardstock (Prism); vintage paper (Jenni Bowlin); flowers, patterned paper (Prima); buttons (BasicGrey); chipboard letters, lace (Melissa Frances); tag (Anna Griffin); adhesive (Glue Dots, Making Memories); Misc: acrylic paint

QUICK TIP

Spray paint is a quick way to alter the color of flowers. Secure a flower to a piece of scrap paper with repositionable adhesive before spraying.

All her friends started calling her Maddi-SUN and now it has become her nickname. I think it is adorable and suits her so well...2008

CRUMPLE AND DISTRESS FLOWERS

My goal here was to create a sparkly yet natural arrangement to go with my photo. Like autumn leaves that have fallen to the ground, I wanted the petals to look like they had been gently walked on. I used a spray bottle to dampen a cluster of various flowers. I crumpled them in my hand then placed them in a paper bag. Using an iron on a low heat setting, I ironed the bag. I scattered the flowers around the page and sprinkled sequins and glitter for some spice.

Supplies: Cardstock (Prism); chipboard letters, flowers (Prima); glitter (Making Memories); adhesive (3M, Glue Dots)

Stitch a vellum quilt

Melissa made a mini-quilt for this page about her baby daughter. This is another beautiful example of how sewing meets scrapbooking with depth and charm. A vellum quilt is a great addition to this page about a precious newborn.

materials

6 large flowers

3 small flowers

6 buttons

cardstock

adhesive

vellum

sewing machine

needle

thread

Supplies: Buttons, flowers, patterned paper, sticker (Making Memories); vellum (WorldWin); flee ce accents (American Crafts); chipboard letters (BasicGrey); rhinestones (Jesse James); Misc: floss

Artwork by Melissa Philips

one

Attach the large flowers to your background cardstock in a grid pattern, two by three. Lay the vellum on top of the flower grid.

two

Stitch the vellum to the cardstock creating a grid with six squares. Stitch around the perimeter of the grid and then in between the flowers.

three

Layer three of the buttons on top of the three small flowers. Hand stitch those to the vellum, over the top of three quilted flowers. Stitch the rest of the buttons to the remaining quilted flowers.

letters + numbers

… Now I know my ABCs, next time won't you sing with me? How many of you used that old song to learn the alphabet? Without letters, we would have a hard time communicating, especially on layouts where pictures don't speak a thousand words. Alphabet and number embellishments are available in a various forms such as cardstock stickers, chipboard, self-adhesive foam, rub-ons and more. But even with the variety of styles and materials, when you use letters on every page, it's easy to fall into the same alphabet routine. Perhaps you have an overabundance of letters in your stash begging for a fresh way to be used. The ideas in this section will stretch your letter stash to new creative heights. And soon you'll find yourself singing a brand-new tune.

Artwork by Judi VanValkinburg

USE THOSE STICKERS—PERIOD

Who doesn't end up with loads of little periods and dots after finishing up a sheet of alphabet stickers? On this layout Judi employed a simple yet very cool idea for making use of the extra dots on her alpha sheet. She simply scattered them around the title to add a little visual interest. It's like doodling with dimension. And it adds the perfect sprinkling of lively color to draw out the blue from the photos. Great design idea!

Supplies: Cardstock (Bazzill); patterned paper (Scenic Route); letter stickers (American Crafts); buttons (7gypsies, Autumn Leaves); frosted swirls (Maya Road); stamp (October Afternoon); adhesive (Glue Dots, Tombow)

DISCOVER A "NUMBER" OF POSSIBILITIES

Can you see the clever way Cindy used number stickers on this page? Several eights resemble petals of the flower, reinforcing the theme of the page while adding texture and dimension. This technique also allowed Cindy to make use of those leftover numbers. Hmmm ... I can just hear your wheels turning at the "number" of possibilities!

Supplies: Button, chipboard letters, lace trim, metal accent, patterned paper, ribbon, rickrack (We R Memory Keepers); number stickers (American Crafts, KI Memories); labels (Scenic Route); brads (Queen & Co.); flower, photo corner (Heidi Swapp); paint (Making Memories)

Artwork by Cindy Tobey

In this age where recycling is reaching global popularity, isn't it fitting to reuse and recycle for our scrapbook pages? On this layout, I wanted to create a transparent title so the photo would show through and remain the focus. Taking chipboard letters and tracing them on a transparency allowed me not only to achieve this look but also to reuse the chipboard letters for another project. I used the same trick to craft my own tags. I printed my journaling on the leftover transparency for a unique way to journal this story.

Supplies: Patterned paper (BasicGrey, Pink Paislee); die-cut shape (BasicGrey); letters (BasicGrey, Rusty Pickle); transparency (Printworks); adhesive (Glue Dots)

materials

chipboard letters

transparency sheet

wide permanent marker

micro-tip scissors

one

Trace a chipboard letter onto a transparency sheet using a permanent marker.

two

Cut out each letter using micro-tip scissors. Cut around the outside of the black lines so that your letters will be visible on the page.

BE IN STITCHES

Not only is tracing your chipboard letters a way to use them endlessly, but the number of ways in which you can use the tracing seems nearly endless too! Jamie's layout is a great example. She traced her letters onto the background paper, and then hand stitched around the the outline of the letters. The hand stitching lends itself to this family page with homespun charm.

Supplies: Cardstock (Bazzill); calendar paper (Teresa Collins); chipboard star, stamps (Technique Tuesday); rub-ons (Scenic Route); chipboard tracers (Me & My Big Ideas); Misc: floss

Artwork by Jamie Harper

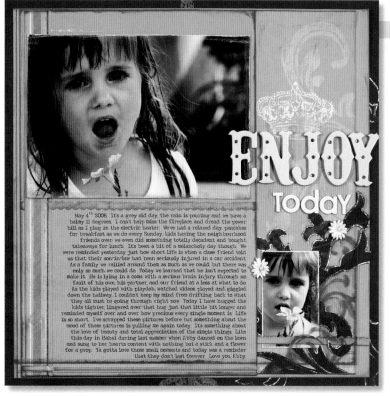

Artwork by Nic Howard

ADD SOME BLING

Chipboard letters with a little bling stand out beautiully on Nic's page about an everyday moment with her daughter. After I saw Nic's page, I began considering all the tiny treasures I could embed in chipboard alphas. Using the technique is as simple as punching holes in chipboard letters, making sure not to punch all the way through. The holes are perfect for resting a gem, small button, pearl or any small piece that fits in the space.

Patterned paper (My Mind's Eye); chipboard letters (CherryArte, Scrapworks); rhinestones (My Mind's Eye); flowers (Prima); scalloped scissors (Fiskars)

Once I find letters I like, I tend to buy multiple sets in various colors because they work so well on my pages. In this case, the different hues inspired me to create a whole new letter in three different colors. I really love how the design of the letters on this layout reinforces the words in my title. Very cool and hip if you ask me!

Supplies: Cardstock; letters (American Crafts, Heidi Swapp); chipboard circle (Urban Lily); adhesive (Glue Dots)

materials

three sets of chipboard letters (same style, different colors)

scissors

one

Gather the three sets of chipboard letters.

two

Cut each letter in three pieces. Be sure to cut the same letters in the same spots.

three

Piece the letters back together. Now each letter should be made of three colors.

Note: It's possible to use three different letters, if parts of the letters are the same. For example, the bottom of this *L* is the same as the top of the *T*.

Dress alphas with decorative tape

letters + numbers

If you have an abundant supply of decorative tape (or even if you don't!), you will find this technique perfect for dressing up your alphas. I came up with this trick, which provides my letters with a customized pattern in no time flat. I prefer to combine embellishments to create my own for a unique design. That distinctive style translated well on this page about my son and daughter's closeness in age.

Supplies: Patterned paper (Dream Street, KI Memories); decorative tape (7gypsies, Heidi Swapp); metal shapes (7gypsies); letters (Rusty Pickle); brads (American Crafts); adhesive (Glue Dots); Misc: buttons, dimensional paint

materials

chipboard letters

4–5 pieces of self-adhesive decorative tape

chipboard sheet

scissors

craft knife

craft mat

one

Set the chipboard letters on the sheet of chipboard. Run several rows of different decorative tape across the letters.

two

Rub your fingernail around the edges of the letters to make an outline of the letter. Cut around the letters.

three

Peel apart the the chipboard sheet backing from the letters.

four

Cut off the excess ribbon tape using a craft knife. When you place your finished letters be sure to line up the design.

Disneyland by

DAY...

...and by

NiGht

I have never been a big fan of Disneyland, but when I look at Sleeping Beauty's Castle I always feel the magic! 03.08

Artwork by Suzy Plantamura

MAKE WORDS SPARKLE

I can't stop gawking at Suzy's genius work of art on these chipboard letters! When she told me how she crafted the designs, I couldn't believe how simple and easy it is to pull off this look. (It's detailed, but not as difficult as it might appear.) First, she painted each letter with a different acrylic paint color. Then she used everyday objects—such as the eraser on the end of a pencil and the edge of cardstock—dipped in white paint as stamps for the designs. Finally, she coated each of these letters with a dimensional gloss medium finish and sprinkled it all with glitter. It expresses the playful, sparkling feeling of a trip to Disneyland!

Supplies: Cardstock (Bazzill); chipboard letters (Maya Road); ribbon (Michaels); rickrack (Making Memories, Me & My Big Ideas); brads (Making Memories, Queen & Co.); glitter (Stampendous); Misc: paint

QUICK TIP

Have you run out of certain letters? You can mix and match letter stickers with chipboard letters and alpha stamps for an eclectic look.

metal

As a mother of two boys, over the years I've often looked to metal as the perfect choice for providing a masculine touch to scrapbook pages. The beauty of using metal is that it's not only gender neutral but it's unexpected and can be altered just as easily as many other embellishments with paint, sandpaper, rub-ons and so much more. Metal embellishments are produced by a variety of scrapbook companies, which makes them a safe choice for your albums. Metal can go beyond basic and being rough and masculine, and in this chapter we will show you a variety of ways to incorporate metal for both your boy and girl pages.

metal

FRAME PHOTOS WITH BOOKPLATES

Judi discovered a clever way to use several metal bookplates from her stash. Framing her photos with the various sizes and shapes is an interesting but easy way to embellish photos. Coordinating brads add even more interest. It's a simple way to put together a clean, graphic design for a layout with photos that really pop.

Artwork by Judi VanValkinburg

Supplies: Cardstock (Bazzill); bookplates (Creative Imaginations, Jo-Ann's, Li'l Davis); brads, rubons (SEI); number stamp (Martha Stewart); letter stickers (Doodlebug); Misc: ink

SHOW OFF PHOTOS WITH BOTTLE CAPS

As Judi illustrated, using metal is a great way to frame photos. Here, Rita took the idea in a different direction, using large metal bottle caps. Plus, the bottle caps provide loads of dimension, matched by the journaling strip adhered with adhesive foam.

Supplies: Cardstock (WorldWin, Bazzill); patterned paper (Scenic Route); bottle caps (Maya Road); flowers, frame, rhinestone swirls (Prima); chipboard letters (American Crafts); glitter paint (Ranger); adhesive (Glue Dots, Making Memories)

Artwork by Rita Weiss

Turn metal into petals

Kimber really "turns" heads with this sweet lay-out about her daughter. She used metal photo turns to stand in as flower petals, perfect for a springtime page. It just goes to show that thinking beyond the obvious always achieves great results!

Supplies: Cardstock (WorldWin); patterned paper (BasicGrey, Creative Imaginations); letter stickers (BasicGrey); metal accents (American Crafts, Creative Impressions, Making Memories); pins (Fancy Pants, Heidi Grace); die-cut paper (Provo Craft); glossy topcoat (Ranger); Misc: ink

Artwork by Kimber McGray

materials

patterned paper

scissors or circle punch

photo turns

pencil

brads

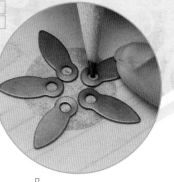

one

Cut or punch a small cardstock or patterned paper circle.

two

Place photo turns around the center of the circle's edges so they are touching. Mark the holes with a pencil.

three

Poke holes in the pencil marks. Attach photo turns to the circle with brads.

This layout is all about the celebration of my son, Fletcher. We held his birthday party at a rock climbing facility, and I wanted the background of my page to resemble the rugged look of a rock climbing wall, pegs and all. I attached assorted shapes and styles of metal to the background and painted them to blend with the background. I love how the technique really brings to life the climbing experience.

Supplies: Cardstock (Bazzill); chipboard letters (BasicGrey); metal pieces, paint (Making Memories, unknown); adhesive (Glue Dots)

materials

assortment of brads, conchos or other small metal shapes

mouse pad (optional)

paintbrush

glitter paint

acrylic paint

one

Randomly place various metal brads and conchos all over your layout's background. Place a mouse pad underneath the background for easy insertion of conchos.

two

Brush a coat of glitter paint over all of the metal pieces.

three

Brush a coat of paint over the metal pieces, allowing some of the background color to show through.

It was finally warm enough to sit outside for our weekly visit to Starbucks.

soda

You enjoyed your usual Clementine soda & I enjoyed the sunshine, my iced tea & taking lots of photos of you.

& SUnShine

Artwork by Cindy Tobey

TAG PHOTOS WITH METAL RIMS

Metal-rimmed tags are another scrapbooking supply staple, and also another example of how well metal works as tiny photo frames for a page. Cindy shows how you can frame your photos, and bits of patterned paper, too, with a series of different shapes to create an art gallery effect. Tying the tags together makes for an interesting twist.

Supplies: Cardstock (Bazzill, WorldWin); patterned paper, ribbon (Prima); metal rims (Making Memories); chipboard letters, letter stickers (American Crafts); stickers (Avery); brads (Around the Block); decorative tape (Heidi Swapp, unknown); adhesive (Kokuyo, Stampin' Up); Misc: staples

QUICK TIP
Using a punch and disposable aluminum pans found in the grocery store, you can create your own custom metal die-cuts quickly and affordably.

PAINT A MODEL EMBELLISHMENT

These photos of my son practicing his spelling words in shaving cream inspired me to create a one-of-a-kind embellishment using metal frames. I wanted the frames to reflect that cool blue swirly mess in the photos, and I accomplished this by mixing paint and modeling paste and brushing it over the frame. I layered the frames over letter-embossed metal to symbolize the page theme.

Supplies: Cardstock (Bazzill); patterned paper (BasicGrey, Chatterbox); letter stickers, metal elements (Making Memories); brass template (unknown); ribbon (Fiskars); adhesive (Glue Dots); Misc: modeling paste, paint, tags

Transfer photos onto metal

I was stunned when I saw this amazing page and then again when I realized Jamie ironed her photo to a sheet of metal to create a truly one-of-a-kind embellishment. Transferring an image to metal provides a vintage quality for layouts, especially when coupled with beautiful, enlarged black-and-white photos. High-contrast, black-and-white photos work best for this technique.

Supplies: Cardstock (Bazzill); brads, date stamp, metal embossed words, metal paper (Making Memories); charm (unknown)

JUL 2002

CHERISH DETERMINATION LOVE
cherish *determination* *love*

Artwork by Jamie Harper

materials

- iron-on transfer paper
- black-and-white photo
- scissors
- thin sheet of metal
- iron

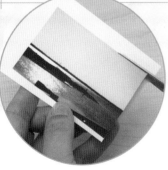

one
Print your photo onto the transfer paper. Then cut it out.

two
Place the photo facedown on the metal.

three
Set your iron to high heat and iron over the back side of the transfer paper.

ribbon

I have been scrapbooking for more than 10 years, and the first time I saw ribbon used on a scrapbook page I remember thinking, "Why didn't I think of that?" It's so logical to include this embellishment in your scrapping because of the variety of patterns, textures and colors. You know you can tie ribbon into a bow and trim a page with it. But how about dressing up circles, making butterflies and piecing patchwork borders? Ribbon is really versatile! Check out just a few of the many ribbon possibilities to get your wheels turning.

Wrap rings with ribbon

ribbon

This is one of my favorite go-to techniques for adding color and whimsy to my pages. Wrapping ribbon around circles or frames or just about any shape I can find allows me to inject pattern, color and texture all in one fell swoop. And for a unique technique, it's super simple to create! Rolls of ribbon work best as you need a fairly long length to wrap whatever shape you choose. But smaller scraps of very thin ribbon can be put to use, too, on smaller pieces like metal-rimmed tags.

Supplies: Cardstock (Prism); journaling circle, letter stickers, patterned paper (Luxe); ribbon (Doodlebug, Luxe); adhesive (Glue Dots)

materials

ring (about 5" [13cm] in diameter)
ribbon (about 28" [70cm] long)
adhesive

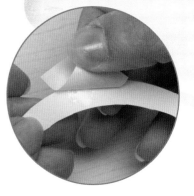

one

Add a bit of adhesive to the back of the ring and attach the end of the ribbon to it.

two

Wind the ribbon loosely around the ring and attach the end of the ribbon to the back of the ring using adhesive.

QUICK TIP

To keep ribbon edges from fraying, use a lighter. Quickly run the flame along the edge of the ribbon. It will melt the raw edge to seal it.

It was Easter Sunday and I wanted pictures of the girls in their new dresses. They would not cooperate and just kept dancing around. I think our pictures were more fun this way!

dance dance dance DANCE dance dance dance dance dance

Artwork by Suzy Plantamura

SCRAP WITH SCRAPS

Here's a creative way to use ribbon scraps left over from projects: Use those scraps, as Suzy has done on this page, to create a patchwork photo frame. The colorful bits and pieces make a bold and bright quilt perfect for highlighting a carefree picture. Plus, this technique is a great excuse for holding on to every scrap of ribbon!

Supplies: Cardstock (Bazzill); rub-on letters (Creative Imaginations); ribbon (KI Memories, Making Memories, Maya Road, Prima, unknown)

TAKE RIBBON TO ANOTHER DIMENSION

On this layout, Nic takes ribbon twisting to another dimension—from flat to fabulously 3-D! Nic brushed ribbon stiffener on to her ribbon and curled the pieces around a pencil. The result are beautiful swirls of ribbon that add an interesting twist on the page. Multiple ribbons are the perfect finishing touch to a page about a sweet little girl.

Supplies: Cardstock (Bazzill); patterned paper (Making Memories, Scenic Route); letter stickers (Scenic Route); brads, felt ribbon, rhinestones (Queen & Co.); brads (Love You More); ribbon stiff (Strano); paper punch (Fiskars); adhesive (Glue Dots); Misc: ink, paint

missing YOU

You've only just turned four, but already I'm feeling sad about you going to school. I love this 4 year old stage! You are the youngest of the kids, you are my last 'little friend' staying at home with me during the day. Miss you already, but making most of your last year as a pre-schooler. May 2008.

Artwork by Nic Howard

Fold a ribbon butterfly

ribbon

What I love about Melissa's layouts is the way she uses soft, feminine touches. This lovely page is no exception. The ribbon butterflies lend a light, whimsical feel to the layout as they adorn the adorable photo of her daughter. With the addition of acrylic, these flights of wonder spring to life.

Supplies: Patterned paper (BasicGrey, Making Memories); bookplate, chipboard letters, scallop border (Prima); ribbon (May Arts, Offray); letter stickers (BasicGrey); acrylic butterflies (Pageframes); stamp (7gypsies); Misc: ink

Artwork by Melissa Phillips

materials

wide sheer ribbon (about 13" [33cm] long)

adhesive

thin opaque ribbon (about 13" [33cm] long)

one

Make a loop at one end of your sheer ribbon. Secure the loop with adhesive. Make another loop next to the first one and secure it.

two

Flip over the loops and rotate them so that they are facing down. Make two more loops that face up. You should now have four loops in an X shape.

three

Wrap the opaque piece of ribbon around the middle of the sheer ribbon X so the two opaque ends are sticking up.

four

Tie the ends in a knot and pull them tight.

Stitch a ribbon bouquet

Kimber stitched her own adorable flower embellishments using scraps of ribbon. Even if you're not a seamstress (like me!) you can create these one-of-a-kind embellishments using any color, pattern or style of ribbon. The ribbon width determines the size of a flower, so keep in mind that the wider the ribbon, the bigger the flower.

Supplies: Cardstock (WorldWin); patterned paper (Making Memories); letter stickers (Reminisce); chipboard shape (ScrapSupply); ribbon (May Arts); brads (Imaginisce); Misc: floss, paint

June '07

while celebrating our neighbor's graduation from High School, you got to take a walk through their beautiful flower garden.

Artwork by Kimber McGray

materials

6" (15cm) length of ribbon

thread

needle

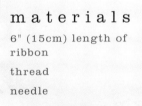

one

Thread your needle and knot the thread. Then sew a loose running stitch along one edge of the ribbon. Start at one end and continue to the other end.

two

Holding the ribbon in one hand and the unknotted end of thread in the other, slide the ribbon down towards the knotted end of thread to gather the ribbon.

three

Fold the ribbon into a circle. Then stitch the ends together. Make sure the ends are folded on the underside of the flower to hide them.

rub-ons

As the name implies, this embellishment is designed for you to rub it onto a surface. Rub-ons lack the dimension that most embellishments provide—but that's exactly their charm. The beauty of this particular embellishment is its ability to be transferred seamlessly onto a variety of materials. Apply rub-ons to wood, vinyl, cardboard, plastic, metal, plaster, paper, glass ... just about any surface you'd like to accent. I dare you to try them all! And try these innovative ways to use rub-ons to enhance your pages.

Rub on a custom pattern

rub-ons

I tend to use just a single rub-on or maybe two on a layout. But I discovered that I can create a custom background design using an entire sheet of rub-ons, even one already missing a few of its images. This technique works especially well with duplicate sheets of the same design, so you can cover a larger area. On this layout, I love how the contrast of the black rub-ons against the white background works with my color photos. But don't count out colored rub-ons. They would create a nice effect as well.

Supplies: Cardstock (Bazzill); rub-ons (BasicGrey); letter stickers (Heidi Swapp, Me & My Big Ideas); brads, eyelets, rhinestones (Heidi Swapp); adhesive (3M, Glue Dots)

materials

two identical sheets of rub-ons
craft stick or stylus

one

Apply the first sheet of rub-ons, starting at the top edge of your background.

two

Rub-on the second sheet at the bottom half of the background. Be sure to align the edges of both sheets.

Artwork by Cindy Tobey

EMBELLISH TITLE LETTERS

Cindy painted her raw chipboard letters and applied a rub-on to the title. She took a rub-on on the same length as her title and placed it over the letters, removing the rub-on pieces that fell between the letters. She applied another layer of paint over the letters to give the rub-on design a more subdued effect. What a fabulous way to dress up a title!

Supplies: Chipboard letters, lace trim, patterned paper, ribbon, rub-ons (We R Memory Keepers); letter stickers (American Crafts); brads, eyelets (K&Co.); chipboard butterfly (Jenni Bowlin); acrylic butterfly (Heidi Swapp); journaling strips (EK Success); adhesive (Glue Dots, Kokuyo); Misc: ink, paint, thread, wire

POP UP RUB-ONS

Though rub-ons themselves are flat, you can still use them to make dimensional embellishments for your page. Follow Melissa's lead: She applied butterfly rub-ons to patterned paper and then cut around the shape. She bent the wings upward to give the butterflies a lift and sprinkled glitter and rhinestones for extra shimmer and depth. You can adapt this idea for any rub-on shape such as flowers, stars and hearts.

Supplies: Cardstock (Bazzill); patterned paper (BasicGrey, Fancy Pants, Making Memories); chipboard tag (Autumn Leaves); rub-on accents (Jenni Bowlin, Melissa Frances); buttons (BasicGrey); flowers, rhinestones (Doodlebug); chipboard letters, letter stickers, ribbon (Making Memories); felt butterflies (Jenni Bowlin)

Artwork by Melissa Phillips

Mix & match rub-ons

rub-ons

Suzy's layout illustrates another idea for using multiple rub-ons on a page. Rub-ons for this technique can be mixed and matched from different sheets. The result of Suzy's easy rub-on technique is a fabulous addition to her page that reinforces her theme and makes her sweet six-year-old the star of the show.

Artwork by Suzy Plantamura

Supplies: Patterned paper (Creative Imaginations); rub-ons (7gypsies, BasicGrey, Daisy D's, Doodlebug, Fancy Pants); acrylic star (Pageframes); chipboard number (Pressed Petals); trim (Melissa Frances, Prima)

Chloe turned six years old this week, but she hasn't really changed much. She is still my sweet baby girl wanting to be held, wanting to sleep with me, and still... crying lots of tears. I hope she stays this way forever! March, '08

one
Trace the acrylic shape onto cardstock.

two
Layer various rub-ons inside the traced shape. It's okay if the rub-ons run over the edges of the shape. If you're adding letters or numbers to your design, rub them on last so they're entirely visible.

three
Cut out the shape just inside the pencil lines. Attach the acrylic shape over the cardstock one.

materials

large acrylic shape

cardstock or heavy weight patterned paper

adhesive

pencil

craft stick or stylus

assorted rub-ons

scissors

Use rub-ons to resist paint

After years of working with rub-ons, I have found that you cannot really change the color on a rub-on because it resists paint. This minor setback turned into a great idea to try a resist technique using white rub-ons and acrylic paint. The paint, when brushed across the rub-ons, resists most of the color leaving you with a saturated background and slightly tinted design. I like that this technique matches the layout's title; it's a twist to the expected.

Supplies: Cardstock (WorldWin); patterned paper (Doodlebug, Reminisce); rub-on (BasicGrey); letter stickers (American Crafts); stamp (7gypsies); chipboard accents (Urban Lily); Misc: flowers, paint

materials

white rub-ons	acrylic paint
craft stick or stylus	paintbrush

one

Rub your image onto the background

two

Paint over it with acrylic paint and allow the paint to dry.

QUICK TIP
You can remove stray rub-on pieces using transparent tape.

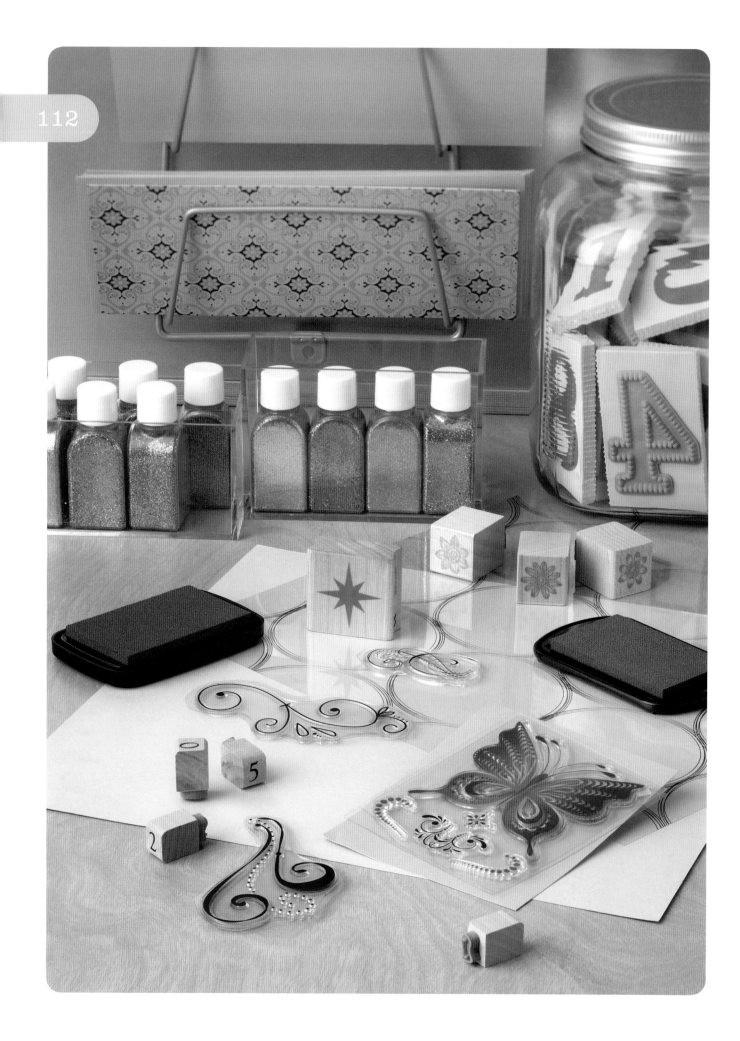

stamps

While stamps themselves aren't technically an embellishment—since you don't actually use the stamp itself on a page—the images they yield make for lots of fun ways to embellish a layout. Mounted, unmounted, acrylic, rubber, self-inking: There are many types of stamps to choose from. Consider all the types of inks—dye-based, solvent, chalk—and it makes for numerous decisions. But with stamps, there's no doubt about one thing: Including stamped images on layouts is a great idea. In this section, you'll discover lots of great ways to stamp your art out in your scrapbooks.

Stamp a background

s t a m p s

Like rub-ons, stamps blend seamlessly into a page. They blend so seamlessly, in fact, that you'll wonder where the stamping even begins. Cindy's subtle work on this page amazes me. The beautiful pattern on the die-cut horse looks like professionally designed patterned paper. But in fact, Cindy made the orange and brown pattern with stamps. Not only that, she used a simple corner stamp to craft a more ornate design.

Supplies: Acrylic and felt shapes, patterned paper, ribbon, stamp (Fancy Pants); chipboard letters (Creative Imaginations, Fancy Pants); brads, eyelets (Making Memories); journaling star (Jenni Bowlin); adhesive (Glue Dots, Kokuyo); Misc: floss, ink, paint, twine

Artwork by Cindy Tobey

materials

ruler

pencil

corner stamp

ink

one

Lightly draw a grid on your paper. Squares in the grid should be about 2" (5cm). If you have a stamp larger than 2" (5cm), then make your squares bigger.

two

Use the grid to align your stamps. Stamp each triangular section surrounding the intersection. The intersection will be the center of your finished, diamond-shaped design.

Artwork by Melissa Phillips

HIGHLIGHT WITH STAMPS

Melissa used stamped images to embellish this adorable baby album. A beautiful stamp frames the title, and a simple circle stamp highlights the calendar month. Stamps are great for dressing up a page, and they also serve well to draw attention to certain features. Highlight a date as Melissa did, or use an arrow to draw attention to a photo or a circle to feature parts of your pattern paper design.

Supplies: Mini album (Maya Road); acrylic stamps (Creative Imaginations, Melissa Frances); buttons, chipboard, glitter, patterned paper, resin accent (Melissa Frances); ribbon (May Arts); metal accent (vintage); adhesive pearls (K&Co.); flowers (Prima); rhinestones (Heidi Swapp); Misc: ink

2 HANDBOOK HOW-TO | **KICK IT UP**
Layer stamped images

I love popping flat elements off the page. On this layout, I layered stamped images for dimension in various places on the page, stamping on both cardstock and transparencies for depth and shine. These stamped images are the equivalent of creating your own die-cuts out of any type of patterned paper—but more fun!

Supplies: Cardstock (Bazzill); patterned paper (Creative Imaginations, Dream Street, Scenic Route); transparency (Hambly); stamps (Inque Boutique); rhinestones (Doodlebug); dimensional adhesive (EK Success); Misc: ink

m a t e r i a l s

stamp

solvent ink

cardstock

transparency sheet

scissors

dimensional adhesive dot

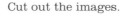

one

Stamp your image on cardstock and on the transparency.

two

Cut out the images.

three

Add a dimensional adhesive dot to the back of the transparency shape and layer it over the cardstock shape.

Artwork by Jamie Harper

GET THE MOST FROM A STAMP

Some stamps really go the distance. Take Jamie's example:
She used a stamp set to create all the elements on her page.
From the background pattern to the title to a place for
journaling, her page is entirely made up of stamped images.
Plus, the black, white and red color combo punches up her
black-and-white photos.

Supplies: Cardstock (Bazzill); stamps (Technique Tuesday); Misc: envelope

Artwork by Jamie Harper

LAYER DIFFERENT STAMP STYLES

If you focus on the star in the center of this wall art Jamie created, you will see that there are layers of stamps working together to embellish the star. Don't be afraid to layer two or more stamps to fashion your own one-of-a-kind work of art.

Supplies: Frame, mat (Jo-Ann's); patterned paper, rub-on word (Scenic Route); chipboard letters (BasicGrey); scallop trim, stamps, star accent (Technique Tuesday); Misc: glitter, ink

QUICK TIP

For a crisp image when stamping, be sure to press the stamp straight down onto the background, press and then lift straight up. Any wavering side to side will distort your image.

Paint a dreamy stamped background

A water bleed technique on a page about fun in the water complements these photos perfectly. The title says it all: Complete and total fun! And that's what Judi's technique provides as well. You will feel like a kid with a watercolor paint book as the stamped image magically changes before your eyes. Of course, a technique involving water works well to enhance a page like this one, but any layout that calls for a romantic or dreamy style would benefit.

Supplies: Cardstock (Bazzill); chipboard flowers, stamps (Technique Tuesday); buttons (Autumn Leaves); Misc: ink

Artwork by Judi VanValkinburg

materials

stamp

dye-based ink

paintbrush

water

one

Stamp the image on your background.

two

Dip your paintbrush in water and then brush over the stamped image so the ink runs.

stickers

Stickers are the tried-and-true embellishment of every scrapbookers' stash. Stickers have been around since the dawn of modern scrapbooking, a staple in every project from grade school sticker books to the early days of scrapping with patterned paper. Perhaps you've traded your stickers for embellishments more modern and cool. I beg you to reconsider! Like any go-to embellishment, stickers come in a variety of shapes, styles, colors and sizes. Naturally, their charm lies in their ability to stick to virtually any surface. The key to spicing up your stickers is to think about them in a new light. Follow me as I show you some ways to "stick it" to the plain ol' average sticker.

1 HANDBOOK HOW-TO | SIMPLY CREATE
Ink sticker edges

To give a sticker some dimension, try this trick that Kimber used on her baby gift bag. Simply ink the edges of the sticker so that it appears to have more depth and contrasts with the background. Who doesn't want a simple way to dress up an ordinary embellishment? Try it the next time your're "stuck" on what to do with your layouts.

Supplies: Gift bag (Michaels); cardstock (WorldWin); patterned paper (Heidi Grace); stickers (Heidi Grace, Melissa Frances); letter stickers (American Crafts); ribbon (Melissa Frances); decorative scissors (Fiskars); Misc: ink

materials

sticker

solvent ink

Ink the edges
of the sticker.

Artwork by Kimber McGray

STICK WITH WORDS TO ENHANCE JOURNALING

Word stickers can enhance the journaling on a layout. Adding a few phrases to highlight heartfelt words spices up your story. On this page, Jamie used stickers to establish the base for the sentimental feelings she wanted to convey about her precious boy.

Artwork by Jamie Harper

Supplies: Cardstock (Bazzill); bracket, chipboard letters, patterned paper, word stickers (Creative Imaginations); stamp (Heidi Swapp); Misc: ink

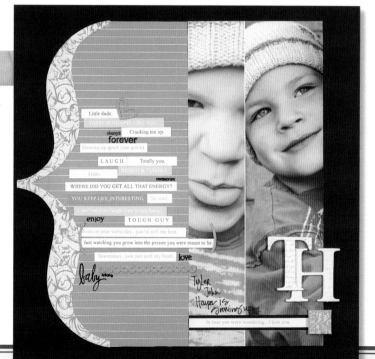

COVER CHIPBOARD WITH STICKERS

Here is another clever way to use up a variety of stickers to embellish your page. Suzy covered a chipboard arrow with stickers of different shapes and sizes. With the chipboard completely covered, she trimmed around the edge of the shape to remove excess stickers. The result is a unique embellishment that dresses up the page.

Supplies: Patterned paper (KI Memories, Scenic Route); letter and accent stickers, ribbon (KI Memories); glossy topcoat (Ranger); Misc: ink, staples

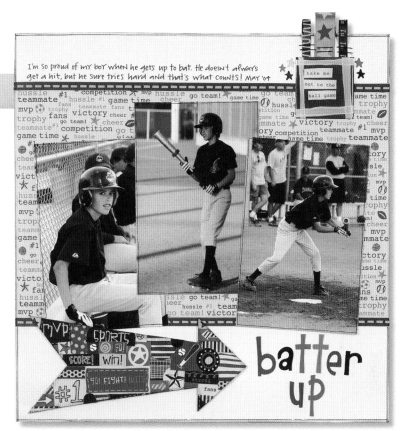

Artwork by Suzy Plantamura

APPLY MEDIA TO STICKERS

Using different media to alter your stickers can transform them into something special. For example, dimensional gloss medium provides shine and dimension, while glitter glue adds sparkle. On this layout, I applied clear embossing powder to create a water effect, which reinforces the theme of my layout.

Supplies: Cardstock (Bazzill); patterned paper (KI Memories, Scenic Route); letter stickers (American Crafts); journaling tag (Fontwerks); Misc: embossing powder

QUICK TIP

To make a sticker repositionable, attach it to a scrap piece of paper and cut it out.

HANDBOOK HOW-TO | **KICK IT UP**

Use stickers as a paint mask

Here, Rita shares a great solution for creating a title with mismatched letters. Just use the stickers as a mask. Once you peel them off the page, you can't tell if they were the same color. What a fabulous idea for all those sheets of leftover letter stickers!

Supplies: Cardstock (WorldWin); patterned paper (BasicGrey); letter stickers (American Crafts); sticker accents (Scenic Route); dimensional adhesive, ribbon (Making Memories)

Artwork by Rita Weiss

materials

letter stickers
acrylic paint
paintbrush
tweezers (optional)

one

Lightly adhere the letters to your background.

two

Paint over the stickers.

three

Carefully peel off the stickers. Use tweezers as needed to lift up the edges.

Give sticker sheets dimension

Stickers by nature are flat, but making them pop on a page is a cinch! Layering stickers with printed transparencies provides some depth. I embellished my entire layout with one sheet of stickers—everything from the title to the decorative elements. The key to this kind of creation is some precise craft knife work and a little help from adhesive foam.

Supplies: Cardstock (Bazzill); stickers (BoBunny); brads, eyelets (American Crafts); transparency (Hambly); dimensional adhesive (EK Success); adhesive (3M, Glue Dots)

materials

craft knife
sticker sheet
adhesive foam
printed transparency

one

Cut around the part of the sticker that you want to pop. Add adhesive foam to it.

two

Layer the background sticker piece over the printed transparency.

three

Layer the piece you cut out (with the adhesive foam) over the transparency.

tags

Do you remember that childhood game of tag? One person touches another and shouts, "Tag, you're it!" When I think of tag embellishments, I am reminded of this game. At one point, tags, traditionally an office supply staple, became readily available in scrapbook stores. And soon after, this embellishment suffered from overuse and was in need of a reinvention. Just like players in the game of tag, this embellishment was not "it" for long. But tags just need a fresh look to reclaim their title. Here's a whole batch of new ideas to have fun with tags.

Gather & paint a tag photo mat

tags

Rita's unique use of tags on this page comes not from what she does to them, but what she does with them. Gathered together, the tag shapes make a wonderful mosaic background for Rita's photos and title. Of course, what Rita did to the tags also enhances the page. She painted each tag and enhanced it with pen work detail. Then she added her photos with colorful clips.

Supplies: Cardstock (Bazzill, Prism); chipboard tags (Maya Road); chipboard letters (Heidi Swapp); flowers (Prima); clips (Making Memories); Misc: decorative tape, paint, ribbon

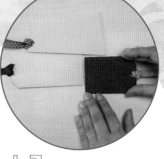

Artwork by Rita Weiss

materials

chipboard tags
acrylic paint
paintbrush
ribbon

one

Brush acrylic paint on each tag. You can stop at one thin coat or apply several coats for a more opaque look.

two

Tie ribbon to the tags.

three

Arrange the tags in a formation that will fit behind your photos.

ARRANGE TAGS IN A FRESH WAY

Have you used a tag as a journaling block? Of course you have. You need something new! Nic shows that by staggering several tags together in a grouping she can fit her story neatly in the tag space and create a fresh design on her page. She embellished her tags with stamping and string to complete the look. Any size tags grouped together works well for this technique.

Supplies: Cardstock (Bazzill); patterned paper (My Mind's Eye, Pink Paislee); tags (My Mind's Eye, office supply store); letter stickers (American Crafts); rhinestones (Kaiser); paper punch (Fiskars); Misc: ink

Artwork by Nic Howard

Artwork by Judi VanValkinburg

PUNCH TAGS INTO ART

Judi added the perfect "punch" to her tags with punch art. Using a die-cutting machine, she cut out the various shapes from her tags to build an adorable border for her page. Handheld punches would work great for this look as well. Notice in the top right corner that her butterfly is partially punched through the tag and the wings are lifted up. This is a fabulous way to add dimension.

Supplies: Cardstock (Bazzill); patterned paper (SEI); die-cut tags (Provo Craft); chipboard letters (American Crafts); eyelets (Making Memories); brads (BasicGrey, K&Co.); adhesive (3M, Glue Dots, Tombow)

Arrange a metal-rimmed border

tags

Making a scallopped border with metal rimmed tags is easily done in just a few steps. My husband is such a kid at heart and I felt the rounded scalloped border would lend a playful feel to the birthday layout. The metal is a masculine touch—a sturdy grown-up feel that balances the playfulness.

Supplies: Patterned paper (Fancy Pants, Scenic Route); metal rim tags (office supply store); numbers (Rusty Pickle); brads (American Crafts); ribbon (Doodlebug); adhesive (Glue Dots); Misc: paint

m a t e r i a l s

craft knife

metal-rimmed tags (about 10)

patterned paper

strong adhesive

one

Using the craft knife, cut out the paper centers of the tags. Then add a line of adhesive to the back side of the edge of the patterned paper.

two

Attach the first tag to the adhesive, hiding half the ring behind the paper and letting the other half stick up. Place the second ring next to it in the same manner. Continue with the remaining tags.

HELP WORDS MAKE AN IMPACT

Metal-rimmed tags, with their paper centers, are a must-have for this technique. Kimber cut the tag and peeled it back giving the illusion that the words are bursting from their centers. This embellishment is perfect for an active, athletics-themed layout because it provides energy and movement. What an appropriately titled page!

Supplies: Cardstock (WorldWin); letter stickers, rub-on letters (American Crafts); metal rim tags (office supply store); brads (Making Memories)

Artwork by Kimber McGray

CRAFT MINI WORKS OF ART

Suzy used her tags as mini art canvases that hold her title. She accomplished this look by decorating shipping tags with torn paper, stamps, embossing powder, inks and rub-ons. The collage effect matches the beauty of her photos and ties the elements together. This is a stunning example of how well tags can enhance a page.

Supplies: Patterned paper (7gypsies, Adornit, Autumn Leaves, Daisy D's, K&Co., Prima); tags (office supply store); rub-ons (Fancy Pants); ribbon (BasicGrey); trim (Melissa Frances); letter stickers (Making Memories); pin (7gypsies); stamps (Hero Arts, Postmodern Design, Stampin' Up); Misc: embossing powder, ink, thread

Artwork by Suzy Plantamura

Artwork by Cindy Tobey

What could better embellish a page about a special gift than tags? Cindy took the idea of using tags to a whole new level when she attached her photo to tags in this creative way. Her title also sits atop a tag to further enhance the theme. This technique will certainly be "it" for quite a while!

Supplies: Chipboard letters and accents, felt shapes, patterned paper (Fancy Pants); brads (BoBunny); letter stickers (American Crafts); ribbon (Fancy Pants, Mrs. Grossman's, Pebbles); tags (Making Memories); cloth reinforcers (7gypsies); paper trim (Doodlebug); adhesive (Glue Dots, Kokuyo); Misc: floss, paint, thread

QUICK TIP
If you don't have tags, you can always make your own. Simply cut out a rectangle from cardstock and punch a hole at one end. Add a reinforcer for added protection—and flair!

materials

tags (about 4)

craft knife

transparent tape

digital photo

printer

transparent label sheet

scissors

one

Using the craft knife, cut out the tags' reinforcers and set them aside.

two

Arrange the tags so they will cover most of the photo. Keep in mind any color on the tags will show through the photo. Loosely attach the tags using transparent tape on their back sides.

three

Print your photo onto the transparent label sheet. Remove the backing and attach the sheet over the arrangement of tags.

four

Cut around the perimeter of the tag arrangement to remove the excess photo.

five

Replace the reinforcers in the tags.

Gallery

Step It up to Extraordinary Layouts

Have you ever started a page and wished someone else would come along and add the perfect embellishments to complete it? The foundation of a page is often the easy part of a layout; sorting through all those gorgeous embellishments can be overwhelming. To show you how embellishments can take your work from ordinary to extraordinary, I asked some friends to help me out. For each of the following layouts, one scrapper created a solid but simple layout and sent it to two other scrappers who each added embellishments to make it rock.

Patterned paper and a single embellishment coordinate with the photo on Katrina's original layout, but the design begged for something more. Rita's additions—punched butterflies, a strip of ribbon and patterned paper circles—provide whimsy and sweetness. I took the layout to another level with glitter and a dressed-up title that make the page shine.

Artwork by Katrina Simeck

STEP

STEP

Artwork by Rita Weiss

15 faves

1. chocolate
2. bend it like beckham
3. soccer
4. pride and prejudice
5. skiing
6. magenta
7. warm weather
8. biology
9. teen vogue
10. the fratellis
11. gilmore girls
12. peppermint hot chocolate
13. summer vacation
14. my ipod
15. pf chang's

STEP

Supplies: Cardstock (Bazzill); patterned paper (BasicGrey, Sassafras Lass); felt flower, rub-on letters (American Crafts); butterfly punch (Martha Stewart); ribbon, silk flower (Prima); brads (American Crafts, Bazzill); die-cuts, letter stickers (BasicGrey); chipboard numbers (Heidi Swapp); journal sticker (Fontwerks); Misc: glitter

gallery

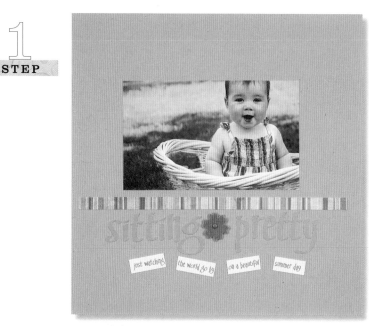

The title for this sweet photo says it all. There is nothing wrong with Katrina's original design, but a few key embellishments that Suzy added enhance the simple foundation. The hand stitching, ribbon and patterned paper photo mat keep the page soft yet take it up a notch. Judi added her own spin with chipboard and felt and more patterns on the background. The resulting fun and playfulness highlight the theme of this page.

Artwork by Katrina Simeck

2&3 STEPS

Supplies: Cardstock (Bazzill, Die Cuts With A View, Prism); patterned paper (BasicGrey, Fancy Pants, Hambly, KI Memories, SEI); die-cut letters (QuicKutz); button (BasicGrey); brad (Jo-Ann's); flower (American Crafts); chipboard (Maya Road); ribbon (BasicGrey, Prima); paper punch (Martha Stewart); adhesive (3M, Glue Dots); Misc: embossing powder, floss, ink, microbeads

Artwork by Suzy Plantamura and Judi VanValkinburg

STEP

Artwork by Stephanie Vetne

Stephanie's original layout in this pair has all the necessary ingredients for a well-designed scrapbook page—a title, journaling and a fabulous photo. What's missing is the pizzazz. Rita's stepped it up with ribbon, flowers and jewels to infuse the page with personality. Stamped images, rub-ons, buttons applied to the center of the flowers and word stickers helped Jamie make this page extraordinary.

2 & 3 STEPS

Supplies: Cardstock (Bazzill); patterned paper, ribbon (BasicGrey); flowers, rhinestone swirls (Prima); stamp (Technique Tuesday); black ribbon (Heidi Swapp); buttons (Jo-Ann's); rub-ons, word strips (7gypsies)

Artwork by Rita Weiss and Jamie Harper

STEP 1

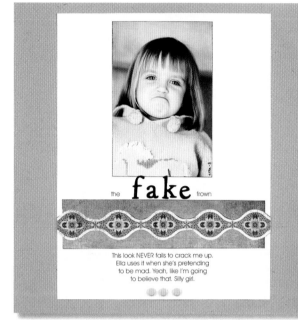

the **fake** frown

This look NEVER fails to crack me up.
Ella uses it when she's pretending
to be mad. Yeah, like I'm going
to believe that. Silly girl.

Artwork by Janet Ohlson

Janet's original layout features an adorable photo with journaling highlighted by a row of brads. A very nice layout, without question, but Kimber's embellishments—a border that separates the title from the journaling and a clip attached to the photo—make it more interesting. Judi's further enhancement of the title and framing of the photo pushed this layout to extraordinary. Just seven added embellishments take the page from good to wow.

2 & 3 STEPS

Supplies: Cardstock (WorldWin); buttons, chipboard accents, patterned paper (BasicGrey, Making Memories); letter stickers (Scenic Route); brads, clip, paint (Making Memories); photo corners (Heidi Swapp); transparent frame (My Mind's Eye)

the **fake** frown

This look NEVER fails to crack me up.
Ella uses it when she's pretending
to be mad. Yeah, like I'm going
to believe that. Silly girl.

Artwork by Kimber McGray and Judi VanValkinburg

STEP

Janet knew this page about her Irish lad and lassie should feature plenty of green, so she splashed on some paint and added a green trim. The original page has spunk, but a little more excitement never hurts. Outlining the shamrocks with some pen work and backing them with orange flowers brings out the kids' hair color. Rita also worked her magic on the title and distressed the paper. These touches reinvent the page. Judi went on to change the journaling to provide more dimension, added patterned papers and positioned that big question mark to draw the eye to the title.

Artwork by Janet Ohlson

STEPS

Supplies: Brads, cardstock (Bazzill); patterned paper (BasicGrey, Scenic Route); paper trim (Doodlebug); letter stickers (American Crafts, BasicGrey); shamrocks by Pattie Knox (Designer Digitals); flowers (Prima); clip (Making Memories); chipboard, ribbon (BasicGrey); journaling tag (Anna Griffin); border stickers (KI Memories); adhesive (3M, Tombow); Misc: paint pen

Artwork by Rita Weiss and Judi Van Valkinburg